Italo-Hispanic Literary Relations

Scripta Humanistica

Directed by
BRUNO M. DAMIANI
The Catholic University of America

ADVISORY BOARD

Italo-Hispanic Literary Relations

Edited by
J. Helí Hernández

𝔖cripta 𝔥umanistica

49

Italo-Hispanic literary relations / edited by J. Helí Hernández.
      p. cm. — (Scripta Humanistica ; 49)
      Includes bibliographies.
      ISBN 0-916379-56-6 : $33.00
      1. Literature, Comparative—Spanish and Italian. 2. Literature, Comparative—Italian and Spanish. I. Helí Hernández, Jesús. II. Series: Scripta Humanistica (Series) ; 49.
PQ6042.I5I84   1989
850.9—dc20   89-35530
          CIP

Publisher and Distributor:
SCRIPTA HUMANISTICA
1383 Kersey Lane
Potomac, Maryland, 20854, U.S.A.

© SCRIPTA HUMANISTICA
Library of Congress Catalog Card Number 89-35530
International Standard Book Number 0-916379-56-6

Table of Contents

Introduction

Along with a renewed interest in the teaching and the study of Romance languages and literatures in North America, the last decades brought on an intensification of interest in the comparative approach. The comparative studies in Romance literatures have consistently increased and critics continue to investigate and analyze further similarities and/or differences, especially between Italian and Spanish literatures.

Today Italy and Spain are indeed two different nations with two different cultures and literatures; furthermore, Italians and Spaniards are very different in their behavior and in their ways of living. But are their literatures totally different? In comparing these two literatures Joaquín Arce, in *Literaturas italiana y española frente a frente* (1982), tries to demonstrate that in their origins, development and artistic preferences both literatures manifest themselves as radically independent and as two different entities. Arce also states that their history, their vital and artistic manifestations, and their psychology do not always move in the same direction. He concludes that very often the close relationships between Italian and Spanish literatures have been exaggerated.

Historically, however, no other two nations in Europe have been in more contact with each other than Italy and Spain. Since Medieval times these two nations have shared a common history and similar cultural and literary productions. Italy and Spain have always revealed a mutual liking and a reciprocal enticement due perhaps to the fact that they feel very interdependent. Each nation finds in the other what seems to be lacking in its own nation. The history and the consciousness of Italy and Spain possess a uniqueness and, consequently, a decisive influence on each other and on the rest of Europe.

1

The literary relations between Italy and Spain are based on their capacity for admiration and reception of their literary works. There is a mysterious and subtle mechanism by which the creative stimulus of one author receives admiration and imitation from another author. The influences seen in this light can be subtlely accepted or consciously searched. for.

Spanish writers have always admired and imitated the literary production of Italy. In *El secretario del rey* (1627), Bermúdez de Pedraza called Italy "*Señora de la pluma.*" The admiration and imitation predominated especially in the sixteenth and seventeenth centuries. Even Cervantes, who claimed originality, could not escape the Italian influence. He owes to the Italians the "novela" form, the idea of reflecting life within the compass of a brief narrative. Some of his Short Stories are reminiscent of the Italian tales in structure and quality. Cervantes' followers carried their indebtedness to Italy much further. Frequently, Spanish authors found in the Italian literary works an inexhaustible supply of plots, themes and form.

Italian influence was not limited to a selected group of writers, genre or period. From Medieval times to the present, Spanish literature has been permeated with "*italianismo.*" The bibliographical references on the subject are copious, but by no means exhaustive. The full extent and full account of the Italo-Hispanic Literary relations are far from being completed. Critics and scholars continue to shed light on these two literatures that are so closely intertwined and identified .

I have gouped here a selection of comparative studies which provide a cross-section of the latest research on Italo-Hispanic Literary relations in North America. The essays examine or re-examine several aspects of their relations and discover new literary links. It is hoped that this collection of studies will give the reader a better understanding of the meaning, significance, and literary value of the works examined.

University of Lowell

Three Hispanic-Sardinian writers: Delitala, Suñer and Zatrillas

Mario Aste

The literature of Sardinia should occupy a relevant place in any discussion about Italo-Hispanic relations, given the historical developments regarding the island from the Middle Ages to the Enlightenment. Sardinia's relationship with the Hispanic world began on the 4th of April 1297 when Boniface VIII gave "Regnum Sardiniae" to James II of Aragon by taking the island away from Genoa and Pisa and the independent Sardinian "Guidicato" of Arborea. At the beginning of the XVIII century with the Treaty of London, Sardinia was given to Austria, two years later the island passed to the House of Savoy and through its association with Piedmont began to gravitate again in the world of Italian culture. The fact that for more than four centuries the "regnum Sardiniae" was part of the Hispanic world is of primary importance in the study of Italo-Hispanic relations.

With the XIII century Sardinia began to use Italian again as the official language of government and communications as it had done in part for several decades during Genoa and Pisa economical and political domination from the XI to the XIII century. From the XIV to the XVIII century the intellectual life of the island started to breath and express itself in Catalan first and later Castillian, due to the effects of the unified Spanish crown. Of the previous Italian influence few things remain, among these there is one *Laudario*, found in 1935 by Damiano Filia at Borutta, a town near the northern city of Sassari.

The gravitational pull toward the Hispanic scene came at the expense of any influence that the Italian world of art and letters would have made. Throughout these centuries of political, economic and cultural domination

3

from outside one aspect of Sardinian culture was never conquered: folklore and language. In fact even in the periods of highest form of cultural domination Sardinian as a language never ceased to exist but continued to be the primary mean of communication throughout the island and at the time was used to express if not the best autoctonous literature at least the one with less foreign influence.

Since the official literature of this period was mostly written in the language of power, it was under certain aspects a literature which reflected the official view of government and not the authentic historical situation of the island. A true free literature, interpreter of the island's reality can be found only in the oral tradition of Sardinian poetry in the vulgar tongue. The Sardinian poet who used the local idiom in his compositions did so as a refuge from the ideological points of pressure imposed by those governing the island. Ideology could be considered dangerous and created several problems for the intellectual if it did not follow the official line. Sardinians as a people seemed to indulge in a lack of participation in the unitary life of a nation, first with the Spanish crown and then with Piedmont and its successor the Italian State. Still today, according to several scholars, the reasons for Sardinian bilingualism and cultural isolation can be found in this lack of full participation with the life of a nation which is considered by many a foreign entity usurping the true nation: "sa nassione sarda". This must be a necessary point of departure at the root of any literary discussion about Sardinia. The notion of a Sardinian nation is a very important one and must be given an extraordinary consideration in any discussion especially about Sardinian literature and culture.

True Sardinian culture until the first half of the XX century was prevalently an oral culture that possessed its own language. This situation was exceptionally aggravated by the fact that the local language, spoken by the inhabitants of the island, was always poor of written texts. Michelangelo Pira is of the opinion that the Sardinians were and are:

> "tagliati fuori dalla comunicazione scritta perché manca un potere sardo. Le isituzioni giuridiche sono scritte in una lingua diversa dalla loro. Al sardo scritto ricorrono soltanto i poeti, le cui esigenze peró sono tanto comunicative, quanto espressive. I tentativi dell'Araolla e del Madau di dare un'autonoma dignitá di lingua letteraria al sardo arrivano quando il sardo ha perduto la sua autonomia globale e incomincia a sentirsi dialetto, lingua povera di poveri, rispetto alla lingua ricca dei potenti venuti dal mare. La prese di coscienza

dell'autonomia, in senso tecnico, della lingua sarda e i tentativi di fondarse un volgare illustre sardo si registrano paradossalmente proprio quando le comunità sarde vedono diminuire la misura della loro autonomia politica. Se si prescinde dal breve periodo dei giudicati possiamo dire che lo scrivere in Sardegna e strutturalmente connesso ad una lingua non sarda. Essere istruiti, essere cioé alfabeti, significa conoscere un'altra lingua. Istruito é, almeno per tutto il secolo scorso e nel nostro secolo, il sardo che sa scrivere e parlare in italiano. Istruzione e cultura, scrittura e lingua italiana, sono per la coscienza popolare la stessa cosa." (Pira 133)

This conclusion that today any Sardinian writer from the XVII century must be studied "sub specie italianitatis" must also be applied to writers of the previous centuries when either Castillian or Catalan were the languages of government, thus the works of José Delitala y Castelvi, Sebastián Suñer and José Zatrillas must be analyzed in this study. They, like many others, had to face the problem of linguistic choice. The language of literature by force had to be not their native one but the one impose over the island. This is common to all Sardinian writers from the XIII century to the present day. The most famous of them was the Nobel Prize winner Grazia Deledda, who chose Italian, still less than a century before her, the linguistic decision made by several authors was in favor of Spanish, which was no longer the language of power because Italian was slowly supplementing it by taking a preeminent position.

From the XVI century up to and including the XVII century, literature in Sardinia was mostly written in Castillian. Poetry, drama and narrative are the most common genres but also religious, historical and didactic works have a relevant place. Some of the Sardinian writers who chose Spanish are: Antonio de Lo Frasse from Alghero with his works, *Los Diez Libros de Fortuna de Amor* and *El Canto a la Batalla de Lepanto* and an additional work, though lesser known *Mil y Doscientos Consejos*, which interestingly enough came to light because Miguel de Cervantes mentions it in his *Don Quijote de la Mancha;* Gerolamo Araolla, from Sassari, wrote *Rimas Diversas* in three languages: the dedication is composed in Sardinian, while the greater part of the text is in Castillian and a third is in Italian; Father Angelo Maria Carta, from Cagliari who wrote *Rimas espirituales* and a Jesuit from Iglesias, Antonio Machoni with his *Arte y Vocabulario de la lengua jule y torrocote* (Madrid, 1732) which is a result of his exploratory and missionary activity in Paraguay. Another poet of prominence is Vincenzo Bacallar (1669-1732) from Cagliari, a member of the Royal Spanish Academy who wrote in defense of absolute monarchy according to the dictates of Divine Right.

The theater in Sardinia was the least developed genre and dramatists of this period include Antioco del Arva, a Sardinian Jesuit who attempted to adopt the techniques of Lope de Vega. He proclaimed himself "el primer Lope Sardo" (the first Sardinian Lope); his work, *El Saco Imaginado,* which in Francesco Alziator's opinion, is a modest but interesting work; Francisco Carmona's with his work titled *Pasión de Cristo Nuestro Señor,* considered to be one of the oldest theatrical works of Sardinia and Antonio Maria Esterzili with the *Libro de Comedias,* a most significant work in religious drama.

The first writer object of this study is Jose Delitala y Castelvi, born in 1624 in Cagliari, a poet, military man and interim Viceroy of Sardinia in 1686, who always served the Spanish crown faithfully and proudly. Delitala typifies the Sardinian writer and nobleman of the times, very much in the image of his Spanish counterparts. Many similarities can be drawn about his life and Garcilaso de la Vega's life; but, while Garcilaso's poetry was inspired by Petrarch, Delitala's verses and works seem to have been stolen from Quevedo. Jose Delitala's work entitled *Cima del Monte Parnaso español con las tres musas castellanas, Urania, Caliópe y Euterpe* appears to contain a surprising technical mastery of verse and is made up of three hundred poems of all types and themes developed with extraordinary perfection and ingenuity.

Published in 1672, *Cima del Monte Parnaso Español*[1] in Delitala's intention, was supposed to have completed *Parnaso Español* of Francisco de Quevedo by supplying the three missing muses: Urania, Euterpe and Calíope. The baroque themes of time, love, religion and history, as outlined by Orozco Diaz in *Temas de Barroco,* are portrayed within the Spanish ambiance. Historical figures of prominence in Spain, along with literary and historical events of the hispanic world, are the protagonists of this work: Wamba, the gothic king, Charles V, El Cid, Don Juan of Aragón, Philip II and many others. José Delitala, with *Cima del Monte Parnaso* (1672) and one *Loa* (1666), Written on the occasion of Charles II's birthday, participates fully in the literary movements of the times, especially with regard to the technical artificiosity and the rhetorical elements of his verses. The inspira-

---

[1]   The first edition of Delitala's work was printed in Cagliari in 1672 by Onofrio Martin with the following title: *Cima/Del Monte Parnaso/ Español/ Con Las tres Musas/ Castellanas/ Calíope, Urania y Euterpe/ Fecundas en sus assumptos, por las/ varias poesías/ De/ Don Joseph Delitala, y Castelvi ecc, Con* Licencia/ En Caller.

6

tional motifs of baroque are always at the fore of his poetry, an example of this is in his sonnet IV from "Calíope", written to describe the small river Rosello that flows through the northern Sardinian city of Sassari:

Prodigio undoso; admiracion de gentes,
Nympha veloz, que en humidos cristales
produzes de una mina doze iguales
bocas de plata en liquidas corrientes:

Todas las maravillas excelentes
fueron del tiempo terminos fatales,
y solo han merecido tus raudales
el hazer sus despeños permanentes

Con quanta gloria tus vezinos viven,
Puesto que a tu hermosura no se igualan
El Tiber, Ganges, Trigris, Tajo y Nilo

Todos tu nombre en marmoles escriven,
Todos tu fama en laminas señalan,
Y todos en Roselo hallan asilo. (Alziator 143)

The first four verses are full of light and movement and possess a clear internal rapidity given their baroque framing, but after that everything is made heavier by hyperbolies and very unusual metaphors, especially in light of the last five verses. The sonnet II of Urania instead is dominated by clear and open images, like:

Purpureos rosiclores de la aurora.
Vencia el sol en su primer oriente,
coronando de luzes su alta frente,
quando los montes con sus rayos dora. (Alziator 143-144).

These verses are reminiscent of some of the most strikingly realistic descriptions of nature written by the major Sardinian novelist of contemporary times, Grazia Deledda. The verses of sonnet XV of "Urania", although rooted in the common poetry of his century, give dignity and equilibrium to Delitala's description of man:

7

Antes de ser, costoso es tu cimiento.
Formado ya, todo su ser ignoras,
nasces llorando, y sin saber que lloras,
te ofrece una prision dulce alimento

Al descollar de tu primer aliento,
en la enseñança huyes de tus horas,
y al verte mas crecido, tus mejores
son tener de el amor conocimiento,

En este error la primavers hermosa,
occioso passas, y en la edad florida,
el fructo es fatigar siempre un cuidado

Ya el tiempo te promete firme losa,
que el tu vejez una inquietud dormida,
y es el ser hombre un miserable estado. (Alziator 143)

This poem possesses a greater than usual number of metaphors dealing with human sincerity as an interplay between the passing of seasons and the ages of man. The fatality of destiny is also another theme touched by Delitala and he does so in a series of poems which deal with the worn out and often repitious themes of love, according to the conventions of the times. There are, though, three verses from Canzone I of "Urania" that should be given particular attention, for his poor rendition of the metamorphosis between self and surrounding nature:

Tengo en el coraçon un Ethna vivo,
y en los estremos soi un monte elado
Que suda de congoxa lo abrasado. (Alziator 145).

or when he imitates Petrarch in the Madrigal II of "Urania":

Zelos que al alma sois tan inmortales,
muerte viva, tormento sin sossiego,
volcan en que se atiça tanto fuego,
hydra donde renacen tantos males. (Alziator 144)

8

Among all these verses there are some rays of light and some strokes of lyricism, for example, sonnet XXII of "Euterpe":

Candidos los iazmines, y las rosas,
con el clavel purpureo si sangriento,
pompa mustia seran de el monumento
de Cloris, sacro honor de las hermosas,

floridas, si ynsensibles mariposas,
sus alas arderan al firmamento
de sus ojos, que ya son escarimento,
de lo que duran las humanas cosas

De su bealdad al mas fragante mayo,
que culto vio Aranjuez en sus pensiles,
ya es de la parca lamentable ensayo

Apenas dies, y siete contó abriles
quando rendida al ultimo desmayo,
fue triumpho del poder en manos viles. (Alziator 147)

If a conclusion can be drawn, it must be said that, in Delitala's poetry, intellectualism overcomes fantasy and the preciousness of concepts with the virtuosity of bookish culture overcomes true lyricism. He possesses all the defects of baroque especially its taste for antitheses, metaphors and conventional analogies. Francesco Alziator, in his *Storia della letteratura di Sardegna*, states that besides all these negative aspects there are:

"taluni momenti felici che non si debbono sottovalutare. Diremo anzi qualcosa di piu: se si paragona l'opera di questo poeta sardoispanico con i molti canzonieri che in tutta l'Europa pullularono durante il secolo XVII, siano questi gongoristi, concettisti, marinisti, petrarchisti o comunque ispirati, la *Cima del parnaso español* ha un suo degno, non secondario posto." (Alziator 149)

The second author in this study is Sebastiano Suñer who like all intellectuals of the times wrote also in Italian and Sardinian. He was born in Cagliari in 1643 and joined as a young man the Scolopian Order. After a short stay in Rome he returned to Sardinia where, even though he had left the religious order, he continued his existence in Cagliari financed by a burse from the Archbishop of the city.

Most of his works are contained in a manuscript of 231 pages[2] and include sermons and poems both in Italian and in Spanish, unfortunately most have been lost and what remains are a few fragments of his collection of verses. One lyric in particular *A la soledad de Maria* has been preserved.

> "Sin esposo, porque estaba
> Joseph de la muerte preso,
> Sin padre, porque se esconde,
> Sin Hijo, porque esta muerto,
> Sin luz, porque llora el sol,
> Sin voz, porque muere el verbo,
> Sin Alma, ausente la suya,
> Sin Cuerpo, enterrado el Cuerpo,
> Sin tierra, que todo es sangre,
> Sin ayre, que todo es fuego,
> Sin fuego, que todo es agua,
> Sin agua, que todo es hielo,
> Con la mayor Soledad
> Que humanos pechos se viero . . ." (Alziator 150)

Undoubtedly the artistry of Suñer on making poetry is recognizable in these verses, especially by his use of popular elements like in the religious poetry of the Italian "trecento". Poetry in Suñer, as in St. Francis of Assisi's *Cantico delle creature* and in the *Laude* of Iacopone da Todi, becomes a mystical desire, an unrelented passion for the spiritual in this world, often too realistic and physical. Suñer's verses re-echo the argumentative and logical progression of Iacopone's lines. The syllogism about man and about God's redeeming love for man are continuously pressing the previously expressed idea in order to produce a new concept, a new metaphor and the next image will shed light to the previous one presented and so on. As in Iacopone' *Fugio la croce*:

> "Fugio la croce, ca mme devore;

---

[2] The works of Suñer are contained in the manuscript titled: Miscellanea variarum rerum scripta a frate Sebastiano a S. Joseph Calaritano, Romae, die VII decembris 1662.

la sua calure non pozzo ortare!
Non pozzo portare si granne calore
che ietta la croce, fugenno vo Amore;
non trovo loco, ca la porto en core;
la sua revembranza me fa consumare!
Frate, co' fugi la sua delettanza,
ch'eo vo chedenno d'aver sua amistanza?
Parme che facci gran villananza
de gir fugenno lo so delettare.
Frate, eo si fugio, ca eo so' firito;
venuto m'e'l colpo, lo cor m'a partito.
Non par che tu sente de quel ch'e' ho sentito.
pero non me par che ne sacci parlare." (Contini 297)

Also in Suñer we see the acquisition of a complex artistic form in structure and dimension, which is reflected even in the language. There is in these verses a search for a mystical encounter with the God head and the rhetorical use of concepts creates a contrastive and dialectical movement which deliver, by means of a humble style, the most ardent and intellectually endowed religious culture of the times. The verses of Suñer, in this light, serve as a vigorous point of convergence of several and different cultures: Sardinian, Hispanic and Italian, finalized in the affirmation of a spirituality which is found in concrete contact with reality and which aspires to the realm of heaven.

His lyric "A la soledad de Maria" is not only inspired to the *Laude* of Iacopone da Todi but also must be linked to the Sardinian *Laudario*, written in Italian, found in Borutta. In this "laudario" placed in the appendix of the *Officium Disciplinatorum Sanctissime Crucis* of the Confraternity of Sassari there are several types of lauds: some are written in honor of the Virgin, other in the praise of the Trinity and the rest in veneration of the Holy Cross. These lauds have the same mystical core and the religious fervor of the Umbrian Lauds of the "duecento" and "trecento" and they show to be inspired by the ascetical franciscan spirit which is based on humility and poverty. One of the best fragments of this "laudario" is the invocation of one of the Brothers to the Virgin and her subsequent response:

"Honorata croce di belli colore
de lo precioso sanguae de nostro signore
grande dolore patí la sua madre
bella avocata de li peccatore

11

Ave Maria vergine pura
quanto dolore patisti in quell'ora
quando vidisti quella lanza iscura
dentro lo lato di nostro Signore.

Nulla persona porría contare
li miei dolori e li miei grandi mali
quando lo vidi nudo ispoliare
pieno di piaghe e de grande dolore.
Tuta la notte andava gridando
per tuta la terra l'andava cercando
non lo trovova l'anima mia
pena sentia e grande dolore." (Alziator 65)

This dialogue though did not evolved in Sardinia as it did in Italian and other European literatures into a higher form of poetry or drama. It remained instead at the state of liturgical ceremony, a dramatic scheme for a procession or a prayer service and an embryonic mystery play. It has in its structure an affinity for much earlier Latin hymns and a later medieval literature intent to instruct and admonish the faithfuls. The contrast between "body" and "soul", the representation of the day of judgement, the human element in God's mystery of Incarnation and redemption, the misery connected to the human experience and the final destruction of sin and death are the themes and motifs of this literature.

In this light we must affirm that these verses of Suñer re-echo in many ways the *Stabat Mater* attributed to Iacopone:

"Stabet Mater Dolorosa
Juxta Crucem lacrimosa.
Dum pendebat Filius
Cuius animam gementem.
Contristatam et dopentem
Pertransivit gladius.
O quan tristis et afflicta
Fuit illa benedicta
Mater Unigeniti.

Quae maerebat et dolebat,
Pia Mater dum videbat
Nati poenas incliti.

Qui est homo qui non fleret.
Matrem Christi si videret.
In tanto supplicio?
Quis non posset contristari,
Christi Mater contemplari
Dolentem cum Filio?" (Dronke 62)

and Iacopones's "Pianto della Madonna" from *Donna del Paradiso*:

"Donna de Paradiso
lo tuo figlio e priso
Iesu Cristo beato.
Accurre, donna e vide
che la gente l'allide;
credo che lo s'occide,
tanto l'ho flagellato.
Con'essere porria
che non fece follia
Cristo la spene mia
om l'avesse pigliato?
. . . .
Succurre, donna, adiuta; ca 'l tuo figlio se sputa
e la gente lo muta:
olo dato a Pilato
. . . . O figlio, figlio, figlio,
figlio, amoroso giglio
figlio, chi da consiglio
al cor mio angustiato?
Figlio, occhi iocondi
figlio, co non respondi?
Figlio, perche t'ascondi
dal petto o' si lattato?" (Contini 297-298)

Suñer like Iacopone writes verses which are sustained by a structure based on the contrast between concepts and elements with a short initial proposition hammered continuously throughout the composition:

"Sin padre, porque se esconde,
Sin Hijo, porque esta muerto.

13

Sin luz, porque llora el sol
. . . .
Sin tierra, que todo es sangre
Sin ayre, que todo es fuego,
Sin fuego, que todo es agua,
Sin agua, que todo es hielo." (Alziator 151)

This poem in its structure though, could also be taken, not so much as a rhetoric elaboration of themes but as an indication of one of the most common forms of baroque aesthetics in poetry. Suñer, in fact, was writing his poetry in the middle of the XVII century and at the height of baroque sensibilities.

In the series of antithetical images Suñer also discovers the importance of lyrical forms which will enable him to link his poetry to the metaphors of a much earlier and pure poetry, like the lyrical ballads and romanceros of medieval Spain. The swift movement of his verses through various plains of consciousness and by the means of images produced in the interplay of light and shadows, matter and spirit, fantasy and reality, open the door for communication to all the senses: sight, touch, hearing, smell and taste.

A poetical image is always a transference of meaning and in Suñer it achieves astounding depth of penetration and sensitivity and by doing so he produces elements of transformation not unlike those found in the poetry of Gongora. This aspect of Suñer to search for melody and musical movements in his verses will give a sensitive and ever fresh response to life. All his images are born free from the physical world as seen by the human mind by linking two antagonistic realms through imagination. His verses are a successful combination of music, energy and color and in this respect they elicit a comparison to the poetry of the Andalusian poet, Garcia Lorca.

In his search for images Suñer goes through a series of dramatic visions of earth, heaven and fire which weigh heavily in the fatality of the ninth hour of Golgotha. This obsession for the practical effects of the repetitiveness of the ninth hour brings to mind the poem: *Llanto por Ignacio Sanchez Mejias* of Garcia Lorca:

A las cinco de la tarde.
Eran las cinco en punto de la tarde.
Un niño trajo la blanca sabana
a las cinco de la tarde.
Una esperta de cal ya prevenida

a las cinco de la tarde.
Lo demas era muerte y solo muerte
a las cinco de la tarde
. . . .
Cuando el sudor de nieve fue llegado
a las cinco de la tarde,
cuando la plaza se cubrio de yodo
a las cinco de la tarde,
la muerte puso huevos en la herida
a las cinco de la tarde.
A las cinco en punto de la tarde." (Borea 170)

Here Lorca expresses nothing but the obsession with the fact of goring death accompanied by the death bell toll: "a las cinco de la tarde", "at five in the afternoon" blows like a monotonous hammer and these words recur after every line, just like Suñer had done in his poem *A la soledad de Maria* by repeating and pounding on the ninth hour. There are in both poems images rich in voluptuousness of insistence and repetition especially about the sense of death and destruction. The death of Jesus, the beloved son of Mary, in Suñer and the death of Ignacio Sanchez Mejias, the friend of Lorca.

Lorca like Suñer passes from the hammering images of the hour to a world laden with symbols:

"Dile a la luna que venga,
que no quiero ver la sangre
de Ignacio sobre la arena

Que no quiero verla!
. . . .
Por las gradas sube Ignacio
con toda su muerte a cuestas.
Buscaba el amanecer,
y el amanecer no era.
Busca su perfil seguro,
y el sueño lo desorienta,
Buscaba su hermoso cuerpo
y encontro su sangre abierta!
. . . . No se cerraron sus ojos
cuando vio los cuernos cerca,

15

pero las madres terribles
levantaron la cabeza

. . . .
Pero ya duerme sin fin.
Ya los musgos y la hierba
abren con dedos seguros
la flor de su cadavera.
Y su sangre ya viene cantando;

cantando por marismas y praderas,
resbalando por cuernos ateridos,
vacilando sin alma por la niebla,
tropezando con miles de pezuñas
como una larga, obscura, triste lengua,
para formar un charco de agonia
junto al Guadalquivir de las estrellas." (Borea 170-174)

This is a world conceived in a dream where man battles the laws of life in the effortless poise of youth. There is in this fatalistic sense of death a recalling to old Spanish poetry and tradition, especially in the verses of Jorge Manrique: "nuestras vidas son los ríos — que van a dar en la mar — que es el morir, 'our lives are the rivers — that end in the sea — which is death.'" But while for Suñer and Manrique the end of this life is the beginning of a new one as in the common faith of mankind that resurrection comes after death for Lorca the individual death is final. Lorca's courage though is forcing the issue of death without any softening veil and provokes a clarifying reaction in the mind of the readers by spurring man to dominate death and to be greater than death itself.

There is in both Suñer and Lorca a desire and concentrated interest in the dynamics of the human psyche by the symbolic expressions which they present with the utmost clarity. They recognized that the substance of poetry derives from the images produced by the unconscious and the recollection of symbols. This recollection becomes obsession and with relentless force pounds in the fantastic walls of memory and by doing so takes on the form of musical composition very much similar to the repeated themes of "Bolero" by Ravel.

The poetical world of Suñer thus encompasses lines of tradition from the words of Italian and Spanish literatures. In his poetry we have the conflu-

16

ence of themes, motifs and images which have developed in two separate worlds of Romance while converging on a third one, Sardinian, which preserved its identity even though it was culturally and linguistically dominated by the two in the succession of historical events.

The third prominent figure of this period of Hispano-Sardinian authors is José Zatrillas y Vico, born in 1648 in Cagliari, who at age 29 published a voluminous novel entitled *Engaños y Desengaños del Profano Amor*, a work believed to be autobiographical and an elogy in verse, in honor of Sor Juana Inex de la Cruz: *El Poema heroico al merecido aplauso del unico oraculo de las musas glorioso assombro de los ingenuos Phenix de la poesia*, published in 1695 one year after her death.

He, like Delitala occupied high political offices and was awarded by Charles II the order of the Alcantara and made count of Villasalto and finally by Philip V marquis of Villaclara. But his fortune changed and in 1707 he was arrested and most probably died in jail during the Spanish War of succession. His major literary work is *Engaños y Desesengaños* which was published in Naples in 1687 and was much admired by his contemporaries. The success of this novel full of baroque elements was such that a new edition was published in Spain. For the reader of today this novel is of little value because Zatrillas lacked the spiritual force of inspiration necessary to make a great work of art. The success is perhaps due on the autobiographical character of the narrative, the political personality of the author and his romantic adventures. This novel, which was analyzed by Giancarlo Mancini[3] has an intrinsic value of its own because it belongs to the Sardinian-Hispanic narratives of the XVII century.

Engaños y Desengaños del profano amor is a novel interlaced with several heterogeneous elements all crafted into a main plot, the love affair between the Duque Federigo of Toledo and doña Elvira Peralta, wife of Don Feliz. This adulterous relationship is achieved through the workings of Federigo's friend, Don Luis de Lara and doña Ines Gonzaga. The narrative is not limited only to the love encounters between the two protagonists but indulges also in other detailed descriptions of the adventures among the minor characters, especially the two procurers. There are also in the novel, according to the baroque taste, a minute recitation of the "academias" which are celebrated to keep the jealous husband of Elvira busy and therefore less

---

[3] His essay on this novel was written as part of the University of Cagliari Literature Studies: "Un romanzo sardo-ispanico del secolo XVII." *Annali della Facoltá di Lettere dell'Universitá di Cagliari*, XV (1948), 91-118.

suspicious about his wife. They give purpose to the logical and philosophical outbursts of Elvira and Feliz' stupidity and naivete.

In the plot and subplots of the novel Zatrillas adds also a series of "moralidades": moral sentences which were placed in pivotal places according to the dictates of the Spanish counter-reformation for the purpose of transforming this general and licentious novel into an edifying and moralizing one. This moralistic purpose though, instead of achieving the literary qualities and dimensions of several picaresque novels as *La Pícara Justina* and *Guzmán de Alfarache*,[4] reduces the efforts of Zatrillas by diminishing the artistic values of *Engaños y Desengaños.*

The works of these Hispano-Sardinian authors were the last hurrahs of the XVII century because the winds of change were already affecting Sardinia: Spanish culture was being replaced slowly at first, but soon very rapidly, by the new one: Italian. The new ideas of the Enlightenment, especially the one creating an independent nation was taking hold amongst the intellectuals. This continued even after the passage of the island to the house of Savoy and helped in shaping a Sardinian nationalistic conscience in opposition to the unifying force of the Italian language. But the results are deceiving because the more intense is the imposition of another language, as with Catalan and Castillian and now with Italian, the greater is the demand for a written Sardinian language, although at this stage it is difficult to pinpoint the date of the birth of a new governmental and narrative Sardinian language, since a poetical one already exists, there is clear and definite demand for it, and this can be traced back to the literary vernacular texts of the XI century.

Literature as a vital element of Sardinian culture given these premises should not, and must not, be limited to poetry in the vernacular, but must include everything Sardinian even though written in a different language, given the historical linguistic perspectives of the island. According to Michelangelo Pira, who has written several essays on the issue of Sardinian bilingualism, Sardinian culture was:

"anche nel passato, quella sia orale sia scritta prodotta dalle comunitá interne ma anche da autori cagliaritani, sassaresi, nuoresi sia in sardo sia in italiano; dunque non soltanto gli *Statuti Sassaresi*, la *Carta de Logu*, le *Carte Volgari* di Cagliari, *il poema sui Martiri Turritani* e tutta

---

[4] This is the thesis of Mancini. Another scholar, Pilia, believes that there is a relationship with the *Decameron* of Boccaccio. See, *La letteratura narrativa in Sardegna*, (Cagliari: 1926), 23.

la poesia in lingua sarda (compresa la traduzione della *Divina Comme-dia* e compresi ovviamente i *Condaghi*) bensì anche tutti i libri e gior-nali scritti dai sardi sulla Sardegna e persino libri e giornali non riguar-danti in modo specifico l'Isola ma che in essa abbiano circolato intensa-mente. O si vuole escludere dalla cultura sarda quel che essa ha espresso o assorbito in lingua spagnola e in lingua italiana?"[5]

The most interesting example of this literature is the hymn written by Francesco Ignazio Mannu of Ozieri, a member of the military estate and a judge of the Royal Audience, *Su patriotti sardu a sos feudatarios*, during the revolution led by Giovanni Maria Angioy in 1794. This song known as "La marsigliese sarda", is a call to armed revolt against the tyranny of the feudal system and an invocation to the people, through his "general will", to give birth to the Sardinian nation. This battle must be fought by all and must be continued until the dream is realized because "cuando si tenet su bentu — es prezisu bentulare" (when the wind blows — it is time to harvest).

Perhaps the most appropriate time for the Sardinian nation was at the turn of the previous century, in the wings of the French Revolution. This, in a historical sense, was the appropriate hour to bring about definite changes in the cultural and national life of Sardinia, but Giovanni Maria Angioy's Revolution was doomed to failure because of complex and multiple causes, most of them rooted outside Sardinia itself. The geopolitics of the time made it impossible for the people of the island to reach their ultimate goal. Linguistic scholars, though, find another reason for this failure: the absence of a common orthographic canon of an aulic and illustrious Sardinian written language. In fact according to Sandro Maxia, this phenomenon exists:

"nell' analfabetismo strumentale di quasi tutta la popolazione, nel limitato sviluppo della stessa lingua parlata e infine 'nella appartenenza delle persone alfabete bilingui ai ceti più elevati (clero e nobiltá) che si servono di una lingua diversa da quella sarda (latino prima, poi spagnolo e infine italiano) per la comunicazione scritta tra di loro; ec-cezionalmente a queste persone alfabete (soprattutto ai preti) accadeva di scrivere in sardo (e generalmente in versi) testi destinati ad essere

---

[5]   Michelangelo Pira quoted by Sandro Maxia in "L'Arte e la letteratura in Sardegna: una chiave di lettura" *La Sardegna* ed. Manlio Brigaglia (Cagliari: Edizioni della Torre, 1982), III, 3.

diffusi tra i sardi monolingui che se li trasmettevano oralmente." (Maxia, "L'arte La Sardegna 2).

This question is still pertinent today, and perhaps more so than in the time of Delitala, Suñer and Zatrillas because the population of the island is more educated and more aware that Sardinian, as stated by Max Leopold Wagner, is a true neo-Latin language with its lexicon, its morphological structure and its syntax. However, the identification of any author to Sardinian literature goes beyond the limited linguistic boundaries of Sardinia and reaches its fulfillment in the identification of the writer to the pre-history and his refusal of historical times imposed by the conquerors of the island and finally in the silent resistance to foreign oppression.[6]

University of Lowell

WORKS CITED

Alziator, Francesco. *Storia della letteratura di Sardegna*. Cagliari: Edizioni "La Zattera", 1954.

Borea, Arturo. *Lorca, the poet and his people*. New York: Cooper Square Publishing, 1973.

Contini, G. *Poesia Italiana: Il Duecento*. Milano: Garzianti Editore, 1978.

Delitala, Jose. *Cima/ Del Monte Parnaso/ Español/ Con Las tres Musas/Castellanas/Caliope, Urania y Euterpe / Fecundas en sus assumptos, por las/ varias poesias/ De/ Don Joseph Delitala, y Castelvi ecc, Con Licencia/ En Caller.*Por Onofrio Martin, Cagliari, 1672.

Dessi, Giuseppe. *Narratori di Sardegna*. Milano: Mursia, 1965.

Dronke, Peter. *Medieval Lyric*. London: Hutchinson University Library 1978.

Filia, Damiano. *Il laudario lirico quattrocentista e la via religiosa dei Disciplinati bianchi di Sassari*. Sassari, 1935.

Mancini, Giancarlo. "Un romanzo sardo-ispanico del secolo XVII" *Annali della Facolta di Lettere dell'Universita di Cagliari*, (XV) 1948, 91-118.

---

[6] This concept of history in a Sardinian sense is well analyzed by Giuseppe Dessí in his Introduction to the volume edited by himself: *Narratori di Sardega* (Milano: Mursia, 1965), pp. 7-8.

Maxia, Sandro. "L'Arte e la letteratura in Sardegna: una chiave di lettura" *La Sardegna* ed. Manlio Brigaglia. Cagliari: Edizioni della Torre, 1982. III.

Pira, Michelangelo. *La rivolta dell'oggetto.* Cagliari: Edizioni della Torre, 1977.

The Influence of Carlo Levi in the Narrative of Gabriel García Márquez

Vincenzo Bollettino

The primary concern of this article will be to provide structural and thematic evidence for relating two major writers of the twentieth century: Carlo Levi and Gabriel García Márquez. The study will deal mainly with three novels, *Christ Stopped at Eboli* of Carlo Levi and *La mala hora (The Evil Hour)* and *Cien años de soledad (One Hundred Years of Solitude)* of Gabriel García Márquez. It is to be noted that this writing will in no way attempt to dogmatically prove the inseparability of these works of art; nor will it forthrightly assert the close reliance of one text on the other. Rather, it will provide enough evidence, through a detailed study of form, tone, narrative lines, characters, stylistic devices and vision of the world, to establish a sequence of parallels for themselves. It is hoped that such a study will not only bring Carlo Levi and García Márquez closer together, but will also shed light on the role, reception, and actual influence of the Italian novel in general on Latin American twentieth century literature.

It is my firm belief that a more serious and thorough investigation should be undertaken to clarify, once and for all, what possible connections exist here; for example, to what extent did Massimo Bontempelli contribute to the formation of Julio Cortázar as a writer; or, what revelations were there in Levi's *Cristo si e' fermato a Eboli* that allowed the Colombian writer Gabriel García Márquez to better deal with his novelistic world after the publication of *La hojarasca (The Leaf Storm)* in 1955. North American criticism, mainly that of James Irby, Emir Rodríguez Monegal, Luis Harss, and Jean Franco has maintained throughout the years that contemporary Latin American novelists owe a great deal to William Faulkner. In fact, this assertion took root upon the publication of James Irby's thesis, *The Influence of William Faulkner on Four Latin American Writers* and Luis Harss' *Into the Mainstream*. Subsequent criticism on the Latin American novel has, indeed, continued to rely on such critical statements to the exclusion of any other possible influence on the Latin American writers.

There is certainly no denying that William Faulkner did, in fact, provide a great deal of the technical know-how for these writers in dealing with the complexities of twentieth-century art. What is in question, however, is whether Faulkner is also the source for their spiritual quest into the historical, social, and cultural realities of Latin America.

It seems to me that William Faulkner's mythical world of Yoknapatawpha centers around the decline of the Compson, Sartoris, Benhow, and Mecaslin families as representatives of the Old South, and the rise of the unscrupulous Snopes family, which displaces them. But Faulkner's world deals with a definite period in history. In it, we witness the life of the region from the days of Indian possession, through the Civil War, down to modern times, Gabriel García Márquez, like Juan Rulfo and Carlos Fuentes, reveals to us a world which longs to have a history, but fails simply because there is great void between its history and universal history. It is in this light that the entrance of William Faulkner into Latin American literature becomes highly suspect. García Márquez's "Macondo" and Juan Rulfo's "Jalisco" are closer to Carlo Levi's "Gagliano" than to Faulkner's mythical "Yoknapatawpha".

The fact that Carlo Levi's literary creation has always been relegated to a secondary position in Italy because of the hybrid nature of his writings, political ideology, and literary undercurrents, has caused the mistake of seeing the work mainly as an indictment of the Fascist regime. In fact, it was to propagate the condemnation of Fascism that Time Incorporated of New York undertook the translation and the publication of *Cristo si e' fermato a Eboli*. Carlo Levi's masterpiece was not only a victim of political interpretations that pleased the American public but also of time. It was treated as a basically realistic work, unpretentious and modest in scope, According to the Time reviewers, the book "had some difficulty conveying the nature of its special qualities" (Levi, 8). To them it was a novel, a memoir, an album of sketches, a study in sociology. Indeed, the novel is all of these things to some degree. Ostensibly, to them it was simply a true account of a year that the author spent in a backward, malaria ridden southern Italian village, Gagliano, in the province of Lucania.

With such critical acclaims Carlo Levi's novel was not only confined to a definite period in Italian history, it was also forced to become a thing of the past. There was never any attempt to see the novel's real import: its quest for the very essence of Italian reality beyond the evanescent and superficial qualities of current events. Even in dealing with Italian neo-realism Italian contemporary criticism does not allot to Carlo Levi's *Cristo si e' fermato a Eboli* its due place in Italian post-war literature. But it is evident that Carlo Levi not only continues the neo-realistic trend in Italian literature already latent in Svevo, Pirandello, Moravia and Vittorini, but also helps draw us into the period in literature when the real is fused with the magical in an attempt to reveal, through linguistic devices, a reality that could encompass the totality of man's world. Seen in this light, Carlo Levi's *Cristo si e' fermato a Eboli* becomes the missing link between Gabriel Garcia Márquez' *La mala hora* and his literary masterpiece, *Cien años de soledad*.

Carlo Levi was born in Turin in 1902, member of a well-to-do Jewish family with strong ties to the Socialist party. In 1924 Levi received a doctorate in medicine and participated actively in the literary magazine *Energie Nuove* founded by Piero Gobetti. This liberal journal, which counted Benedetto Croce among its collaborators, leaned strongly toward Croce's idealism. Piero Gobetti, to whom Levi was attached, had previously founded *La Rivoluzione Liberale* in 1922. Gobetti's death in Paris in 1926, at barely twenty-five years of age, profoundly affected Carlo Levi.

Because he now openly aided the Italian socialists in escaping from Italy, Levi became an enemy of the state. In 1934 he was arrested and accused of being a member of the movement "Giustizia e Liberta'". In 1935 he was again arrested and sent into exile in southern Italy. His stay in Grassano and Gagliano ended in 1936 when he was freed during a political amnesty. While in Florence between 1941 and 1943, Carlo Levi began to write *Cristo si e' fermato a Eboli*, which he finished in seven months.

Carlo Levi gained entrance into the artistic world during his formative years as a painter. In 1923 his paintings were exhibited in Venice along with those of Morandi, Carra', Sironi, and Tosi. Piero Gobetti was the first to see in Levi's works a certain arid aspect which was a reaction to the rhetoric of the times. Other art critics noted a hidden spiritual yearning for a simpler and enduring reality. Levi's search of the past, for the memories, and for the essential, became more evident, however, in "Quaderno di Prigione", still unpublished, but cited by Aldo Marcovecchio in *Galleria*, which appeared in 1967 and was completely devoted to Carlo Levi:

July 14, 1935
Isolated from men, I take refuge in the images, I recall the memories of

24

a past that seems full of light as a proof of life, an objective certainty that the present could not give me. But, can I really talk of a past, of a present or of a future? All here is enclosed in this point: laws are shattered so is the idea of time, Nothing moves, all repeats itself identically motionless in itself, the natural movement of things as the past and the future are reduced to an instant in time without any dimension; therefore, not even the present seems to exist because it has no beginning that preceeds it and an aftermath that is born and that which happens while it happens already became motionless and a vague memory. Everything is in it (memory) and in it identical (Marcovecchio, 21).

What is evident in this short passage written by Levi in 1935 is his unhappiness with present realities and events. But the concern expressed here is that of a man who is aware of certain political and social realities and feels obliged to participate in them. Although sensing himself isolated, Levi finds personal solace in taking refuge in the past. This escape, in turn, will allow him better penetration and comprehension of the world of the South of Italy.

As a journalist, Carlo Levi is always objective and politically engaged; but this posture has always been accompanied by a subjective and personally intimate line throughout his career as a writer. The fusion of commitment and personal feeling is accomplished in *Cristo si e' fermato a Eboli,* The fusion of the two narrative lines will account for the novel's unique structural properties.

The external narrative line, objective, historical, and chronological, is the structure most visible and easily approached by the reader. It deals with an historical account of Levi's period of exile in Lucania. From its center Levi will widen his horizon, incorporating into the narrative political, social, religious, and cultural facts. The internal emotional line is lyrical in nature, subjective, impressionistic; it goes above and beyond the empirical observable social reality. Its movement is dynamic, it has a time and a space of its own that are not visible to the naked eye. It arises to the surface only when the reader, through the aid of an image, a sound, or agesture, is able to experience, with the help of intuition, an awakening to a world never seen before.

One can ascertain that a socially and politically oriented reading of *Cristo si e' fermato a Eboli* not only would fail to bring to light the essential "etimon" of the work but would also fail to envision the intimacy existing between the external realistic world and the ever-moving profound reality that the author was able to capture. The reader is the only one who can provide the connective bridges between the double structure of the novel. His presence is a must for the work to acquire meaning and existence. Language therefore is used by Carlo Levi as a revelatory tool of certain historical, cultural, social, and economic realities that govern a town that grows to become the symbol of a group of people, their history and inner reality.

Gabriel García Márquez is, perhaps, the most acclaimed Latin American writer of today. His writings serve as an example of the complexity and maturity of Latin American narrative. His works depend, much as in Levi, on the inventive power of language, which is creativity by language and within language. Such is the dependency on language that the resources of standard criticism fall far short of expectations.

Both Carlo Levi and García Márquez center the existence of their novels in the vitality of the language itself. These characteristics so vital to the "gestalt" of *Cristo si e' fermato a Eboli* appear to be noted tendencies in Gabriel García Márquez from 1962 until 1967, that is from the publication of *La mala hora* until the appearance of *Cien años de soledad* in 1967. García Márquez's *Cien años de soledad* is seen by Latin American critics as an example of the transformation of regionalism in Latin American literature. They see *Cien años de soledad* as Colombian, Spanish American, or as completely universal. However, all of Gabriel García Márquez's cyclical novels (*La hojarasca, El Coronel no tiene quien le escriba (No one Writes to the Colonel), La mala hora,* and *Cien annños de soledad)* have their roots in a very specific period in Colombian history, and one of their characteristics is a persistent need and desire to come to grips with the historical and social events of that time. However, just as in *Cristo si e' fermato a Eboli,* the total historical experience of the novel is transformed upon penetration into the dynamics of those events.

Cristo si e' fermato a Eboli, La mala hora and *Cien años de soledad* make use of pre-Christian and pre-Hispanic mythology as well as contemporary cultural particularities in developing a complicated notion of evil—sacrifice—redemption; mythology—legend—history. Both García Márquez and Levi also insist on the novelist' s right to recreate reality so that both novels are in some way a creation within a creation. To put it in another way, both Carlo Levi and García Márquez assume in their work's the posture of a God who enjoys observing the act of reinterpreting reality.

Both authors are adventurers in technique and tend to stress both the communication of concepts and the lives of the characters. In one way or another, language takes on special values in these two novels with *Cristo si e' fermato a Eboli* playing the most intricate game in this respect. Given their realistic and historical nature, it is important to note that the regional base is vital to both novels.

What is it, in substantive facts, that brings these two writers together? What are the assumptions for such a comparison in structure, thematics, and characterization? Gabriel García Márquez was born in Aracataca, Colombia in 1928. Aracataca, much as Gagliano, is an isolated village supported mainly by the banana plantations owned by the United Fruit Company. The people in Aracataca have no dreams about restructuring society. They have seen countless foreign companies exploit their land and innumerable revolutions, which despite their promise have only made their lives more miserable. They deplore dictatorships. They send their children away to Europe where they think they are better off. The old rebellious spirit of the peasants, however, never dies. Underground papers circulate at night and during the unbearable heat of midday.

Aracataca ceases to be the dilapidated town founded and exploited by the banana companies as soon as García Márquez oversteps the boundaries of reality. He renames the village Macondo. Both realistic and mythic, it becomes the "etimon" of Latin American civilization. Macondo and Gagliano have shared a common history. Now they share an even more common destiny.

In Levi's Gagliano, as in García Márquez's Macondo, there is no way to tell truth from rumor or fantasy. The sloth, credulity, isolation, feudalism, atavistic forces at work, as well as the magic, superstitions, casual sexual openness, and violence are all pointedly and sardonically revealed. In Macondo and Gagliano there are many marvels which have nothing to do with our commonplace scientific world at all; nature does not function there with the regularity or impartiality it shows elsewhere, and time, if it moves at all, moves in circles. Gagliano and Macondo are lost worlds, an anachronistic society at once decadent and magical, amusing and cruel to a sophisticated eye.

Besides drawing a common geographical, cultural, and economic background, Carlo Levi and García Márquez also share common political views. They are both marxists. Their messages however, are quite different. Carlo Levi's Gagliano has its own existence, laws, and reality that stand above those of the rest of the country. García Márquez's Macondo has no existence of its own. It is in search of one. Macondo stands detached not only from universal history (that history shared by the ruling powers) but also from its indigenous roots. It is a world whose umbilical cord was cut prematurely. It

27

was never destined to grow, to acquire a form and thus an existence and a place in the dynamics of universal history.

Such are the historical and cultural facts that bring together the Gagliano of Carlo Levi in *Cristo si e' fermato a Eboli* and the Macondo of García Márquez, ever present in all of his novels. Such physical and historical isolation is the fundamental cause of the deep loneliness that envelops the protagonists of their works of art. In fact, the force and recurrence of this theme is justified by the title of Gabriel García Márquez's major novel: *Cien años de soledad*.

The basic concern of this study is to provide both biographical and literary evidence that would link García Márquez's novelistic world to that of *Cristo si e' fermato a Eboli*. It is known that Gabriel García Márquez was, indeed, acquainted with Carlo Levi's works. (In a brief conversation I held with him in New York at Columbia University, (1969) where he was to receive an honorary degree, he admitted having common grounds with Carlo Levi). It is also known that from 1952 through 1954 he lived in Paris and Rome. In 1954 García Márquez enrolled as a student at the center of experimental cinematography in Rome. This was the period of neo-Realism in the Italian film industry. Carlo Levi's *Cristo si e' fermato a Eboli* was to the Italian filmmakers more than a guide for their search and portrayal of the Italian south. García Márquez, who began to write *La mala hora* after his three-year stay in Italy, published the novel in 1962. His journalistic experience and the cinematic techniques learned in Rome became his new tools in dealing with the novel from that point on. Moreover, the cinematic technique of externally visualizing events and characters drew him ever closer to the novelistic world of Carlo Levi.

In taking García Márquez's cyclical narrative as a whole, one begins to notice a change in style, devices, focus, and structure from his first novel (*La hojarasca*), published in 1955, to his later novels which appeared in 1961 (*El coronel no tiene quien le escriba*, and *La mala hora*). Somehow between 1955 and 1962-67 García Márquez's vision suffered a change—it matured.

La hojarasca published in 1955, is itself a short novel and a complex one. William Faulkner's hand lies heavily upon it in the use of interior monologue, flashback and internalized narrative enveloped in darkness and fatalism. In the novel, three narrators—father, daughter, grandson— sit for half an hour in a room where a doctor, much hated in Macondo, has hanged himself. The town, once prosperous, is now decaying with its bedrooms full of lizards and its silent people devastated by memories. But it is this doctor's sins and omissions, his relations to the family watching over the coffin, that are the matter of this story in which essential details are only grudgingly revealed. The narration proceeds by bits and starts depending, much as in Faulkner, on the sensation evoked. Each crucial scene must be retold before the truth becomes clear. García Márquez is much more concerned with the complex techniques observed in Faulkner than with the social and historical forces that were to occupy him in his later novels.

It becomes clear, then, that the person who might very well have shown García Márquez the way out of the internal morass of *La hojarasca* was Carlo Levi's *Cristo si e' fermato a Eboli*. García Márquez eventually realized that the way to discover the essential reality of Latin America was through its history. *La mala hora* is thus a novel built on social and historical documents. In following the author's own observations, through certain key political incidents, through dialogue among the main protagonists of the town, we learn, often by indirection or intuition, much of the deep significance about Colombian mores and their psychic roots in the nineteenth and twentieth centuries.

La mala hora, Cien años de soledad, and *Cristo si e' fermato a Eboli* are novels in pursuit of the essential reality. Gagliano and Macondo are microcosms of the development of much of the Latin American continent and of Italy: both strange, pristine, fecund, doomed lands where magic fuses with the most poignant realism, where alien values are introduced to subvert the innocent and to infect society with a mortal disease.

Having met Carlo Levi, Gabriel García Márquez realized that the key to the essential reality of Latin America lay not through external observation and through detailed descriptions of milieu and characters alone, but through the amalgamation of realistic exactitude and fantasy. Levi discovered in his exile in southern Italy an underlying reality that had not changed at all since pre-Christian times. García Márquez with the aid of Carlo Levi would discover that the note of wonderment and exoticism since the letters of Columbus and through the chroniclers of Cortéz, Cabeza de Vaca, Garcilaso de la Vega, el Inca constituted a living presence hidden beneath the rubble of modern industrialization that had been forcedly imposed by European history.

Carlo Levi's dictum, and that of García Márquez, would be that the reader must put aside everything he has known until now. Every subject, idea, thought and symbol must be eliminated so as to allow this new, magical reality to spring forth, to catch us by surprise. In each novel, the very first line throws the reader into a timeless flux and/or the unconceivable, freighted with dramatic suspense.

Both *La mala hora* of Gabriel García Márquez and *Cristo si e' fermato a*

29

Eboli of Carlo Levi deal with the political situation of their respective countries. In Levi's Gagliano, the two contending parties are the landowner and professionals (Fascists) and the peasants divided among socialists and the politically unconcerned. The historical period encompasses a period of twenty-one years, from 1922 till 1943.

La mala hora of García Márquez is set in the years of bloody civil war between the Liberal and Conservative parties. Four of more separate phases can be cited in this period, but it is sufficient to point out two major phases of great violence. The first occurred between 1946 and 1953, affecting most of the country, while the second took place between 1954 and 1958, and was limited mostly to the heartland of Colombia. Efforts to find a monolithic cause for the phenomenon of this violence have been successful, though they range from the Freudian to the sociological (Dix, 3). What began as a basically partisan dispute— the wish if the new in-party to consolidate its power and the equally fervent desire of the newly ousted former power-holders to regain their status—escalated into a nightmare far beyond the control of the parties.

Like Carlo Levi in *Cristo si e' fermato a Eboli,* García Márquez does not dwell on the violence alone, but on the state of terror, the misunderstandings, the lack of communication between the two groups that stemmed from cultural and philosophical differences as noted in Mario Vargas Llosa's "*García Márquez: Historia de un deicidio* (Vargas Llosa, 4).

In a period of political calm between elections, the people of Macondo are shocked by the sudden appearance of anonymous pasquinades relating intimate details about the private lives of the town's leading figures. Bit by bit the reader perceives that the appearance of pasquinades underlies a condition of continual disquietude in Macondo. *La mala hora* delineates a culture where hatreds, suspicions, and superstitions are passed on from generation to generation, As Vargas Llosa puts it:

> By its magnitude the violence, fear and mistrust have bored deeply into that society, they are in the air which the people breathe, they constitute an essential trait of the "pueblo". (Vargas Llosa, 135)

Like Carlo Levi's *Cristo si e' fermato a Eboli, La mala hora* sides with neither party. García Márquez, himself a socialist, obviously believes that the problems of the town have roots deeper than the mere differences in nomenclature which distinguish the two parties. Both Levi, and García Márquez suggest that the cause of these problems are to be found in the historical and cultural anomalies present in both societies. They question the validity of the present social, historical, cultural, and economic structures. Thus, while *Cristo* and *La mala hora* can be considered political novels on the surface, each raises a provocative and profound philosophical question: is the present reality one which is intimately related to the people of Gagliano and Macondo?

The search for the essential begins in both novels through a detailed study of the central figures. Thus, the priest, the town mayor, the chief of police, the doctors, the dentists, the pharmacist, the party leader, the lawyer, the landowners, the barber, the maid, become the focus of attention of both writers. In both *Cristo si e' fermato a Eboli* and *La mala hora* they form a constellation, providing us not only with realistic portrayal of town life in a definite historical period, but also with the connective bridges to a magical reality that lies underneath the chaos and the violence.

It is in the portrayal of these characters that García Márquez's debt to Carlo Levi's *Cristo si e' fermato a Eboli* becomes most apparent. It stands to reason, howerver, that the choice of setting also accounts for obvious and natural similarities. In any small village the people in power take the roles mentioned. Their attitudes, dreams and aspirations will also be determined to a great extent by the physical nature of the locale. However, it is not in the choice of the protagonists and locale that we sense and intimate relation between Carlo Levi and García Márquez. It is the range of similarities in the philosophical posture of each protagonist, his allusions, and his positioning in the constellation of figures that one finds thought-provoking.

Both Gagliano and Macondo are isolated villages, far removed from history and from current events. Gagliano is "that other world, hedged in by custom and sorrow, cut off from History and the State, externally patient, to that land without comfort or solace, where the peasant lives out his motionless existence on barren ground in remote poverty, and in the presence of death" (Levi, 8).

Macondo of *La mala hora* is also isolated from civilization. Between the town and the outer world there is a "thick, immobile river" (García Márquez, 40). In *Cien años de soledad*, at that time "Macondo was a village of twenty adobe houses, built on the bank of a river of clear water that ran along a bed of polished stones, which were white and enormous, like prehistoric eggs. The world was so recent that many things lacked names, and in order to indicate them it was necessary to point" (García Márquez, 20).

Carlo Levi says of the people of Gagliano "We're not Christians". They say, "Christ stopped short of here, at Eboli". "Christian" in their way of speaking means "human being" (Levi, 1). In Macondo we sense the same feeling of inferiority, of desolation and abandonment. In *Cien años* the town is an island completely surrounded by water. The description of the atmosphere is also one of boredom, intense heat, where the flies and the rats reign supreme: "The air was black with thousands of flies, and other thousands covered the walls; an old dog was stretched out on the floor with an air of infinite boredom" (García Márquez, 45). The same boredom and a sort of disgust, born of the experience of injustice and horror, were reflected on the widow's pale faced" (García Márquez, 2). In *La mala hora* "Trinidad pushed open the street door and went to the corner where she had set the traps for the mice" (García Márquez, 3). "There was an intense smell of pigeon filth," (García Márquez, 3). "There were flying ants in the clean air" (García Márquez, 4).

After setting the reader in a world forgotten by time and history, and beset by boredom and loneliness, intense heat, constant rains, and violence, both authors move to the center of life in the villages: the square. There, Carlo Levi describes the impenetrable silence: "The village square struck me as more remote and lonely than ever; no echo of the ouside world penetrated so far; no strolling players or peddlers came to break the monotony" (Levi, 11). In *La mala hora*: "The desolate square, the almond trees sleeping in the rain, the village motionless in the inconsolable dawn, produced in him a feeling of abandonment" (García Márquez, 3). In both Gagliano and Macondo there are terrible prophecies. "This village", says one of Levi's protagonists, "in a few years will have ceased to exist; it will all be carried away" (Levi, 11). In *La mala hora* an old wandering woman states: "After all's said and done, the world is coming to an end this year. Blood will run in the streets and there won' t be any human power capable of stopping it" (García Márquez, 148).

Unlike the predictable array of stock figures previously mentioned, García Márquez's village priest is a singular protagonist; yet, he bears the strongest resemblance of all to Carlo Levi's priest in *Cristo si e' fermato a Eboli*. Both men act as the central figure who draws all the others together. They are both bitter, lonely, objects of ridicule. Tormented by the viciousness of the townspeople, they feel helpless as spiritual leaders. Disgusted by his futility as a spiritual leader, Don Trajella's thin lips were turned down "in an expression of habitual bitterness". García Márquez's protagonist bore "a feeling of frustration that tormented him during the evil hours of his life" (García Márquez, 96). Their only escape is through literature. Father Angel of *La mala hora* writes interminable letters to an unknown person.

The church in Gagliano and in Macondo has ceased to have any force or function. The priests, well aware of the townspeople's contempt, are perpetually drunk, lazy, and given to flights of imagination. In Gagliano, "The church was merely a large room with plastered walls, dirty and neglected, with an adorned altar on a wooden platform at one end and a small pulpit on the side" (Levi, 16). According to Levi's Don Trajella, "there's no grace of God in this village; no one comes to church but the boys, and they come to play. I say my mass to empty benches. The people are not baptized" (Levi, 97). In *La mala hora* the church is dilapidated. It is totally invaded by rats: "That night, after rosary, Father Angel found a dead mouse floating in the holy water font" (García Márquez, 165).

The mayor of *Cristo si e' fermato a Eboli*, Luigi Magalone also has his counterpart in *La mala hora*. He is the cruel "alcalde" (mayor) who suffers from an interminable toothache. "Luigi Magalone was only an elementary school teacher and his chief job as a mayor was to watch over the political prisoners sentenced to compulsory residence in Gagliano" (Levi, 40). There are also Dr. Milillo and Dr. Gibilisco, whom the peasants in Gagliano liken to donkeys.

The figure of the doctor in *La mala hora* is as mistrustful of the peasants and the priest as are the doctors of Carlo Levi. In a conversation with Father Angel of *La mala hora*, Dr. Giraldo tells him: "Father: one of these nights put your hand on your heart and ask yourself if you're not trying to put bandages on morality" (García Márquez, 165).

The figures of the barber and the tailor in both novels have the function of spokesmen for the townspeople. In their shops there are frequent political meetings of radical nature. In the figure of the lawyer's lover in *La mala hora* we see a trace of Giulia of *Cristo si e' fermato a Eboli*, but this memorable and timeless protagonist is destined to play a greater role in *Cien años de soledad*.

The figure of Trinidad, who lives with Father Angel in *La mala hora*, is seen in the many maids whom the protagonist of *Cristo si e' fermato a Eboli* encounters. The blind, wandering old woman of *La mala hora* can easily be related to that of the ageless cemetery guardian in Carlo Levi. *"The widow of Asis"* in *La mala hora* also has her counterpart in Luigi Magalone's wife. They represent the matriarchal power in Gagliano and Macondo.

The flute player with whom Carlo Levi shares his lodgings in Gagliano also appears in *La mala hora*. They are both out-of-townels. Their presence constitutes the only link that these two isolated and infernal villages have with the outside world. That connection is established through music. They both disappear from the village. Carlo Levi's protagonist, a tax collector, was chased out, his wife threatened. Pastor of García Márquez is killed after playing the most beautiful melody ever heard in Macondo.

With their disappearances Gagliano and Macondo are left to dissipate. The rain falls heavier than ever, and chaos reigns to such a degree, that Gagliano and Macondo are literally hell on earth. The two protagonists who now command our attention are Baron Turunno, a symbol of the old feudal power in the south of Italy, and Don Sabas, the landowner and money lender of *La mala hora*. Finally, *Cristo si e' fermato a Eboli* closes with one of protagonists exclaiming: "No one ever got this far and we are not expecting anyone in the near future" (Levi, 269). *La mala hora* ends with Father Angel closing the door of the church. That night: "Father Angel couldn't eat. After curfew sounded he sat down to write a letter, and he was leaning over the desk until after midnight while the thin drizzle erased the world around him" (García Márquez, 181). As the cyclical structure of the novel comes to a close, the reader knows he has only received a fleeting glimpse of a reality that stands inextricably out of time and space.

Having adopted Levi's revelations of the archaic and pagan traditions of the Italian South to Macondo, and finding the fit perfect, García Márquez will now be able to begin what should, perhaps, be considered the greatest novel ever to come out of South America in the twentieth century: *Cien años de soledad*. It is a remarkable work of art, where memory and prophecy, illusion and reality, are mixed and made to look the same. Thanks to the novelistic techniques which the Colombian writer inherited from William Faulkner, James Joyce, and Virginia Woolf, he will be able to bring to the surface what in *Cristo si e' fermato a Eboli* remained hidden beneath the apparent in Carlo Levi's social, political, and historical criticism.

What binds *Cristo* and *La mala hora* intimately is the profound need to know the real Italian or the real South American. Indeed, Carlo Levi and García Márquez think of Faulkner's imaginary Yoknapatawpha County in the very terms in which they consider the real Gagliano and the real Macondo—that is as microcosms capable of rising above the economic desiccation and the moral disintegration inherent in capitulation before progressivism. Levi and García Márquez both regard materialism as an alien force destructive of their world.

Carlo Levi's *Cristo si e' fermato a Eboli* is not to be taken simply as the encounter of the civilized North with the primitive South. Nor is García Márquez' *La mala hora* merely an account of the bloody civil strife of 1953 and 1958. Rather, both novels are utter denials of contemporary reality and values and heartfelt affirmation of certain universals born out of the true bond between man and nature, reality and fantasy, individualism and collectivism. *Cristo si e' fermato a Eboli* revealed to García Márquez the need to bring to light that essential reality that has remained intact and untouched by the historical and the social vicissitudes of both countries. This unprecedented attention was destined to cause in both Italy and South America a reappraisal of certain present and past values, and was to lead, in fact, to the rediscovery of certain truths pertaining to their histories.

Carlo Levi was largely concerned in *Cristo si e' fermato a Eboli* with finding the ultrareality that exists beyond or beneath the political chaos brought about by the Fascist regime. García Márquez questioned the ill-assimilated and forcibly imposed Spanish religion, language, thought, modes, culture and history. Latin America could never be made to achieve a new identity after all. God never truly arrived there either; he was only brought by the Spaniards to punish those who did not embrace the power they inveighed in His name. Again, Latin Americans were forced to learn a language that fell far short of their spiritual needs. Once their speech became enslaved by that of the newcomers, they were subverted and infected.

To unveil the hidden essential reality he seeks, then, García Márquez has to distort his medium of expression; he cannot use the very Spanish which is at issue here. As in Carlo Levi's *Cristo si e' fermato a Eboli*; the greatest gift García Márquez offers in *La mala hora* and *Cien años de soledad* is his crisp, rich, and versatile prose. His talent for *le mot juste*, his sensual, striking imagery, the flow of natural and sometimes grotesque humor— all combine to achieve a subtle, psychologrcal penetration into the novels' characters. Most memorable about Carlo Levi's and García Márquez's protagonists is the inexorable solitude in which they exist. Notwithstanding their great anxiety to live fully, to love, dream, and undertake grand enterprises, they are destined not to grow, not to achieve a form or a history or their own. *Vis a vis* universal history, Macondo and Gagliano are microcosms of great cosmic allegory; they are sattrical accounts of the history of Latin America and of southern Italy.

The period of exile in Gagliano provides for Carlo Levi both the motivation and the opportunity to search for the absolute. Nevertheless, it is an ordeal which takes the form of a spiritual descent and final ascent, and which involves a series of trials; for Carlo Levi must first divest himself of Northern Italian influences, definitely western, that impede his entrance into the magical world of the "cafoni" (peasants) of Gagliano. There, time and space have remained stubbornly attached to the reality of the pagan Greek world.

Gabriel García Marquez, also forced into exile from his native Colombia because of political beliefs, encounters a history that is totally alien to his own. García Márquez's exile, much as that of Thomas Mann in *Doctor Faustus,* is largely responsible for the structure of *Cien años de soledad.* Both authors felt a deep need to remain attached to their countries through a reinterpretation of their history.

One device that makes Marquez's narrative work so good is a mastery of the fictional use of history. His protagonists (the Buendías) in their eccentricity, mythical nature, and in their clear historical setting, bear a close resemblance to Carlo Levi's saga of Gagliano in the Italian South. In both there is the recognition that, if handled with the appropriate distance, history can be rendered as an active character in the novel. But while the magical world of the peasant in *Cristo si e' fermato a Eboli* has a reality of its own with time non-existent, in García Márquez the history of Macondo merges with a larger character, time-passage, and this becomes one of the major preoccupations of the characters, if not the major motif of the novel. There is a fascination with time—its linearity, its cyclical quality, and the hypnotic arresting of a single moment. All the Buendias are given similar names, so that the reader gets a feeling that each repeated moment is also the same moment.

Gagliano and Macondo are both taken as small gardens of Eden. One after the other the great inventions and eras of history find their way into the villages, until the parade stops with the Fascist period of 1922 till 1943 in Gagliano, and with the civil war of 1958 in Macondo. History, at this point, departs somehow embarassed and deflated.

Carlo Levi's most useful companion in his existential quest of the essence of the South of Italy was language. He returns to the bare crudeness of speech that carries within it that ancient reality that is closer to myth than to history. Language, therefore, becomes a useful intermediary between the author and the people of Gagliano, between the past and the present, realism and magic realism. Because the word often (assumes the image of sounds and colors displayed and heard in nature), there is a recurrent use of certain words, such as "velo" (veil), "chiave" (key), "chiuso" (closed), "brusio" (indistinct murmur) "immobile civilta' (motionless civilization) "stagno" (pond). Of this world, Carlo Levi is only able to capture fleeting, superficial and undefined images through an impressionistic language based entirely on visual and auditory sensations:

From the dead man's house came the wails of women. An indistinct murmur spun around me in wide circles; beyond lay a deep silence, I

36

felt as if I had fallen from the sky, like a stone into a pond" (Levi, 10).
"Life in Gagliano was a closed world" (Levi, 21). "In some mysterious
way they helped me to penetrate that closed world, shrouded in black
veils, bloody and earthy, that other world where the peasants live and
which no one can enter without a magic key" (Levi, 14).

The list is interminable for it holds the key to understanding *Cristo si e'*
fermato a Eboli, It is through language that Carlo Levi begins his descent and
ascent to the white villages of southern Italy, much as García Márquez does
across the successive periods of the history of Latin America. García Márquez
descends to the souls of his ancestors and villagers, while Carlo Levi
descends to the energetic center of nature and the mythical worlds of the
peasants of Gagliano, certain that they guard the secret entrance to the realm
of the real and the fundamental of Italy.

The Italian author places great importance on the word, especially upon
those words which are particularly revealing because of their power to
penetrate that absolute reality denied to us by reason and by the external veil
of history. This sort of super reality, hidden in words such as "veli neri" (black
veils), "filtri" (love potions), "precipizi di argilla bianca" (steep slopes of white
clay), "strega contadina" (witch-woman), "la donna-vacca" (cow-woman),
"l'uomo lupo" (the werewolf), "il Barone-leone" (the lion baron), "la capra-
diavolo" (the goat-devil), "le donne regine-uccelli" (the women queen bees),
"monachicchi" (gnomes), is actually to be found in nature, in the very relationship between man and things. It is from this unique relationship that the
fantastic springs forth in Levi's novel.

García Márquez's *Cien años de soledad* also abounds with the same
mythical figures: Melquíades the gypsy who came back from death, children
with pigtails (niños con cola de puerco) or the ageless woman Pilar Ternera,
who comes straight from Giulia Venere of Carlo Levi, and who fills Macondo
with illegitimate children. José Arcadio, the first son of the Buendías, is sex-
ually powerful. His closest relative is the "American" in Carlo Levi who is also
known for his virility. There is also the "mulata adolescente con sus teticas de
perra" (the adolescent mulatto with breast of a dog), Santa Sofía the woman-
dog, the man with the sexual organ of a monkey— Nigromanta, the prostitute bleats like a mountain goat. There is Petra Cotes, the woman-rabbit (la
mujer-conejo); Jose Arcadio Buendia, who is determined to discover the
ocean, and to find how to make gold and photograph God; Rebecca, who
eats dirt when she is depressed; Remedios, the beauty who kills anyone who
dares to look at her. There is also the wandering Jew, the priest who prac-

tices public levitation stimulated by nothing hardier than a cup of hot chocolate; the founder of Macondo, who was tied to a chestnut tree and refused to die, is reminiscent of Levi's guardian of the cemetery, who goes back and forth from life to death in Gagliano.

In fact, what is evident in this short list taken at random from both *Cristo si el fermato a Eboli* and *Cien años de soledad* is the close association of both novels through the constant comparison of the world of their protagonists to that of magic and the animals. Notable, as well, is the use of word-symbols which serve as connectives between the villages' inner history and outer civilization, or even between the world of mankind and that of the creatures:

> "The indefinable guardian of the cemetery had a prominent breast-bone like that of a bird, It was said that in the winter he could either make the wolves come down into the villages, or keep them away as he wished. People said that when he was young he wandered over the mountains followed by savage wolf-packs" (Levi, 67). "Giulia Venere's eyes had whites with blue and brown veins in them, like those of dogs. She had sparkling, wolflike teeth. Her face as a whole had a strongly archaic character, not classical in the Greek-Roman sense, but stemming from an antiquity more mysterious and more cruel, which had sprung always from the same ground, and which was unrelated to man, but linked with the soil and its everlasting animal duties, She had the small black head of a serpent. Her lover was a young albino with the pink eyes of a rabbit" (Levi, 105). "Pilar Ternera had become tired of waiting for him (her lover) always identifying him with the tall and the short, blond and brunet men, that her cards promised from land and see within three days, three months or three years, With her waiting she had lost the strength of her thighs, the firmness of her breasts, her habit of tenderness, but she kept the madness of her heart in tact" (García Márquez, 20).

Outside history, routine and conditioned life has obliterated this magical reality for contemporary man to the point of becoming totally fantastic. Secular people such as Giulia Venere, Pilar Ternera, Úrsula, the guardian of the cemetery, Petra Cotes, and Remedios la bella are endowed with magical sensations and revelations representative of a world whose existence is ignored by many. But this new domain cannot be approached via the imagination or psychological relationships; it is only reached by flashes of intuition which recognize no time limit.

We have seen through the analysis of the main characters of *Cristo si e'* *fermato a Eboli, La mala hora,* and *Cien años de soledad* that a definite relationship does exist between the novelistic world of Carlo Levi and that of García Márquez. The plentiful parallels in characterization, structure, motifs, language and vision are not coincidental. Yet García Márquez's imitation is not subservient. Our task is simply to suggest that Carlo Levi's *Cristo si e' fermato a Eboli* might very well have served as a point of inspiration and departure for García Márquez's novelistic world from *La mala hora* to *Cien años de soledad.* If for Carlo Levi the entrance into the square of Gagliano marked the beginning of the crucial search, the probe into those very realities that constitute the physical, psychological, and spiritual being of an Italian, in García Márquez the creation of Macondo is also the search for the essential Latin American reality that he has hidden beneath foreign superimposed Spanish culture and history.

Listening to conversations and studying allusive descriptions of certain key town personalities (Dr. Milillo, Dr. Gibilisco, the mayor, the Fascist leader, Don Trajella, the priest, Giulia Venere, the maid, Don Pasquale the landowner, the gravedigger, the "American" and the barber) we attend a parade of Italian history, traditions, and philosophical truths of an indeterminate time. Gagliano is the very history of Lucania and that of the region is the very history of Italy. Conversely, though Gagliano has suffered the lengthy parade of different periods of Italian history and civilization, it has stubbornly remained attached to a pre-Christian civilization.

Through the Macondo of García Márquez's novels also parade the distinct periods in history that compose Colombia's civilization. From the historical Macondo of *La mala hora* we travel back in time to see the Biblical Macondo, where no one has yet died. With the Spaniards' invasion came bloodshed and death; the seeds of Macondo's eventual downfall were sown. It comes finally in 1958, when a train loaded with thousands of dead people shot at a labor rally against the government moves silently towards the sea.

One of the themes that fuses *Cristo si e' fermato a Eboli* with the narrative of Gabriel García Márquez is the wonder and strangeness of a region in the South of Italy and a whole continent in the South of the Americas in which the fantastic becomes the normative once the external veil of universal history is removed. It is in such a world that Giulia Venere gave birth to seventeen children by seventeen fathers and García Márquez's protagonist, el Coronel Aureliano Buendía, fathered seventeen of his own, all marked with a cross on their foreheads.

Montclair State College

39

WORKS CITED

Dix, H. Robert. *Colombia: The Political Dimensions of Change.* New Haven: Yale University Press, 1967.

Franco, Jean, *The Contemporary Novel and Short Story.* Cambridge: Cambridge University Press, 1969.

García Márquez, Gabriel. *La hojarasca,* Buenos Aires: Editorial Sudamericana, 1969,

_____. *El Coronel no tiene quien le escriba,* Mexico City: Biblioteca ERA, 1963.

_____. *La mala hora.* Mexico City: Biblioteca ERA, 1966.

_____. *Cien años de soledad,* Buenos Aires: Editorial Sud-americana, 1967.

Harss, Luis. *Into the Mainstream. Conversations with Latin American Writers.* New York: Harper and Row, 1969.

Irby,James. *The Influence of William Faulkner on Four Latin American Writers.* Mexico City: Biblioteca ERA, 1966.

Levi, Carlo. *Christ Stopped at Eboli.* (Translated from the Italian by Frances Frenaye), New York: Time Incorporated, 1964.

Marcovecchio, Aldo. *Galleria,* 3/6 (1967).

Rodríguez Monegal, Emir. *Narradores de esta América.* Montevideo: Editorial Alfa, 1960.

Vargas Llosa, Mario. *García Márquez: Historia de un deicidio.* Barcelona: Barral Editores, 1971.

Pantalone Hispanicized:
The Comic Father Figure
in Lope de Vega's la francesilla

Nancy L. D'Antuono

By the last quarter of the sixteenth-century Spanish drama was, as Edwin Morby indicates "a groping, many directional activitiy, potentially fruitful, but without clear orientation. What was missing was a polarizing agent to sift, organize and give direction" (265). It is at this juncture that the *commedia dell'arte*[1] comes to Spain[2] bringing with it those constitutive elements which, in the hands of Lope de Vega, would mark the contours of Spanish Golden Age comedy for the next one hundred years. These components were: 1) a quickpaced, tripartite intrigue centering on the tribulations of young lovers who, with the help of astute servants, overcome the obstacles to their marrying and 2) balance and duplication in characterization and plot to the point that not only are the lovers united at the end of the play, but all unmarried couples on hand are similarly joined.

Lope de Vegas debt to the *comici* for the evolution of the comedy of intrigue and to the *zanni* for the development of the *gracioso* is generally acknowledged.[3] The absorption of other masks, on the other hand, has re-

---

*An earlier version of this paper was presented at the Golden Age Drama Symposium, University of Texas-El Paso, March 12, 1986.
[1] For the origins and development of the *commedia dell'arte* see Ancona, Petraccone; Duchartre; Lea; Apollonio; Nicoll; Pandolfi; Smith; Oreglia and Molinari.
[2] For data corroborating the performances of the Italian players in Spain between 1545 and 1603 consult Pellicer; Sánchez Arjona; Rennert; Díaz de Escobar; Shergold "Ganassa" and Falconieri "Historia".
[3] See Place; Shergold "Ganassa", *History;* Falconieri "Historia"; Arróniz

ceived little attention primarily because they are less easily identifiable. Such is the case with Pantalone. This is due in part to the changes demanded by the adherence of the Spanish *comedia* to predetermined standards of morality and decorum. Tied as these were to national ideals of honor, Church and monarchy, they mandated the attenuation of two of the *commedia dell'arte's* salient characteristics: its bawdiness and its satirization of the upper classes. A respectable Spanish stage father could hardly engage in the comic doings and libidinous pursuits of a Pantalone, much less be the butt of jokes at the hands of an Arlecchino or a Pulcinella. Yet Pantalone is readily discernable in Lope's theater, especially in the early plays, once we are sensitized to those aspects of the mask which remain in the Spanish counterpart.

Unfortunately, this avenue of investigation has been largely overlooked and/or discouraged for a number of reasons. Critics prefer to concentrate on those plays which are widely accepted as being among the best of Lope dramatic production. Little attention, if any at all, is paid to those comedies in which the performance potential outweighs literary merit. Tied to this stance is scholarly inclination to treat Golden Age comedies as literary relics exclusively, with only a passing nod, often begrudgingly, to the role of non-verbal components in the elaboration of the works. Lastly, the elusive nature of the *commedia dell'arte* itself (an atextual theater whose only remains are some 700 *scenari* and a few treatises by actors of the trade) renders the concretization of its impact difficult—but not impossible. My own investigations in this area suggest that the lessons learned from the *comici dell'arte* inform Lope's theatrical technique to a greater degree than is generally acknowledged. This is not intended to negate Lope's innate artistry but rather to call attention to those non-textual elements which stimulated the *Fénix's* extraordinary talent. The pages which follow will shed additional light on the matter by examining the characterization of Alberto, the father figure of *La francesilla* (1596) and its link to the mask of Pantalone. A preliminary review of the basic characteristics of the mask and its incursion into Spain will offer the background necessary for the fullest appreciation of Lope's recasting.

We rarely encounter a *scenario* that does not show Pantalone (or a variant of the mask) at the head of the list of characters; most begin their action with his entrance (Nicoll 44). Pantalone is the classic, wealthy Venetian citizen. Although he is at base an authoritarian father, the mask allows for multiple variations of character and name, thus enabling the individual actor

---

208-309; Listerman "La *commedia dell arte* and "Some Material Contributions"; D'Antuono "Lope de Vega" and *Boccaccio's Novelle* ch. 5.

to leave his unique stamp on the role. On the positive side, Pantalone is a sharp businessman. His values are solidly *bourgois*. These standards are, in turn, ridiculed as Pantalone consorts with servants and ruffians in the pursuit of love and related amusements. On the negative side, he is avaricious and miserly. He is cantankerous, subject to explosive reactions in the face of difficult situations and given to swearing and vituperation when his wishes are contravened. His children are more of a bother than a blessing. For Pantalone "a marriageable daughter is as perishable a commodity as fish" (Lea, 1:20). "His greed is surpassed by an even greater vice, that of lust" (Oreglia 78). In this capacity he becomes the "vecchio scioccamente innamorato, oppure padre destinato alla burla" 'the foolish old man in love or father destined to be ridiculed' (Pandolfi 1:297). His erotic impulses, especially toward very young women often places him in the position of rival to his own son. Lastly, Pantalone's credulity blinds him to the schemes of his children or those of his wife by whom he is often cuckolded.

Red and black are the colors of Pantalone's costume: red tights and a red, close-fitting jacket, a black, wide-sleeved robe (*zimarra*), usually lined in red, a black round hat or a red woolen Greek cap, and black slippers. Occasionally he wears yellow slippers in the Turkish style. Pantalone wears a dark-brown half-mask with prominent, arched eyebrows and a hooked nose. Lower facial makeup includes a long moustache (kept in motion by constant grumbling) and a jutting, pointed beard. He usually wears a short dagger at the waist (for scenes of revenge), a handkerchief (for tearful recognitions) and often a pouch placed in such a way as to suggest a phallus. The iconography in some instances shows a rather prominent phallus, no doubt a survival from the theater of Antiquity (Oreglia 80).

The advent and popularity of the mask of Pantalone in Spain is linked to a single name, that of Stefanello Bottarga, who performed there between 1574 and 1584. Theatrical documents confirm Bottarga's performance in Madrid in 1583 (Shergold, *History* 188). A notarial entry of 1584 attests to the presence of "Estefanelo Botarga" in Seville as one of the actors in charge of the Corpus Christi presentations (Sánchez Arjona 70). Two documents suggest that Stefanello Bottarga may have arrived in. Spain in 1574 with the acting company of Alberto Naselli, alias *Zan Ganassa*.[4] One of these is the single extant speech from Ganassa's repertory, in use before 1573. It is en-

---

[4] The success of Ganassa and his troupe is affirmed by contemporary Spaniards who were, in general, resentful of the attention and earnings Ganassa commanded. See Arróniz 216. For details regarding Ganassa's life see Rasi; Cotarelo y Mori "Noticias" and Falconieri "Más noticias".

titled "Lamento di Giovanni Ganassa con Micer Stefanello Bottarga suo pa-drone sopra la morte di un pidocchio" "The lament of John Ganassa with Messer Stefanello Bottarga his master over the death of a flea' (Shergold "Ganassa" 363).[5] The persistence of the Ganassa/Stefanello Bottarga rela-tionship in Spanish minds is confirmed in a letter of August 1, 1618 from Lope de Vega to his patron, the Duke of Sessa. Alluding to his own sexual continency of late, Lope remarks "Le podríamos decir lo que Ganassa a Estefanelo cuando se le cayó la braqueta, 'patrón, a pájaro muerto, abrille la jaula'" (Shergold "Ganassa" 363) 'We could say what Ganassa said to Stefanello when the fly of his trousers fell open: "Master, for a dead bird, open the cage"'. From the contrapositioning of the names Ganassa and Bot-targa, or Ganassa and Estefanelo, as in the documents just noted, scholars have concluded that Bottarga, like Ganassa was not the name of the actor, but of the mask, in this instance an alternative or double of Pantalone (Lea 11:482). If Stefanello Bottarga used any other name on or off the stage, it has not come down to us.[6]

The impact of both masks on Spanish culture as figures called *ganasas* and *botargas* has been well documented (Shergold "Ganassa"; García Sanz; Caro Baroja). The figures appear in festivities, processions and tournaments from 1590 to the present day century.[7] After 1600 *Ganasas* disappear in name from the festival tradition, leaving the *botargas* who slowly begin to assume the patch-covered, loose pants and blouson of *Zan Ganassa* and his family of comic servants. By the eighteenth century the Italian origin of the *botargas* had been completely forgotten and they were assumed to be part of pre-sixteenth-century folklore (365 n. 6).

The *Diccionario de Autoridades* (1716) corroborates both the fusion (*botargas* dressed *alla ganassa*) and the assumption that "*botarga*" belongs to

---

[5]   The lament was included in Cesare Rao's *Largute e facete lettere*...Nuovamente ristampate, Vicenza, 1585, 98-99 as cited by Shergold "Ganassa" 363, n. 7.

[6]   Goulard 205, n. 52 suggests that the name of the character "Tofano" in Flaminio Scala's *scenario, Li duo vecchi gemelli* may be an alternative rendering of Stefanello. Goulard also notes that Scala's *La Mancata fede* reads "Pantalone, poi nel fine Stefanello Bottarga" 'Pantalone, then at the end, Stefanello Bottarga'. Similarly, the cast for *Il Portalettere* includes "Pantalone, poi Stefanello" 'Pantalone, later Stefanello'. The two notations suggest that Stefanello was enough like Pantalone to be mistaken for him until the final scene. I am indebted to Matilde Goulard's article, the focus of which is the semantic evolution of the Spanish word *botarga*, for the clarifica-tion and confirmation of many details on the subject.

[7]   On *botargas* in the twentieth century see *García Sanz; and Caro Baroja "A caza de botargas"*.

ancient Spanish tradition. (The translations of the dictionary entries are mine.) It offers five acceptations of "botarga," the first being "that part of a suit worn in ancient times which covered the thigh and leg and was wide. It might be called a 'long boot' ("bota larga') for it began at the waist and reached the ankle." The documentation offered as evidence as the following verses from Quevedo's Musa VI, Romance 17, written in 1648:

> The Cid went about those days
> more handsome than Gerineldos
> with a red botarga
> in the figure of a pepper

The humor of the lines has escaped the eighteenth-century compiler, for he fails to recognize the reference to Pantalone's red suit of clothes.

The second meaning points to the fusion and variation noted by Shergold (366). "It commonly refers to what is today called a 'vestido ridiculo' which serves as a costume, of one piece, slipped on from the legs, then the arms, and buttoned with fat buttons. It is made of various contrasting colors...". Can this be anything but the clownish garb of zanni, be he Ganassa, Pulcinella or Pierrot?

The third acceptation notes that "botarga" applies also to the person who wears such garb in mummeries and skits. Here again the compiler misses the mark. The burlesque verses "...that hairy vest with which you were born a "botarga" is a recollection of Pantalone's close-fitting jacket.

"Botarga" is also associated with "a goatskin filled with air and dressed as a soldier wearing a mask, used to provoke the bulls at festivals. It is commonly called 'a tumbler for bulls'. Its base is usually weighted so that it will fall backward when hit and immediately spring up." I am reminded at this point of Giacomo Oreglia's description: "The actor who plays the part of Pantalone must be good at ridiculous backfalls, his reaction to the receipt of bad news or startling revelations (80).

Lastly, "botarga" signifies "a sausage stuffed with pork meat and tied in short lengths, as in longaniza, ...but much tastier and richer" (600).[8] As for modern dictionaries, all repeat the above meanings except for the reference

---

[8] Covarrubias's entry for botarga reads "Latine botulus; cierta especie de longaniza, fit enim botulus ex suilla carne, in farctis intestines, dictus a bolis, id est frustulus carnis quibus ist imbutus (232).

45

to "long boot." Only Joan Corominas (1:501-502) and Maria Moliner (1:406) relate the word to Stefanello Bottarga.

Italian dictionaries associate "bottarga" exclusively with food. They concur that the word is of Arabic origin, from *butarih* related to the Greek *tarichos* or *salagione*, the salting of mullet or tuna roe which is then processed and sun-dried or smoked, being an appetizer similar to caviar. Battaglia's *Grande dizionario* (2: 329) adds: "the word gained currency in the Mediterranean...and penetrated European languages during the sixteenth century (in Italian it is documented in a carnival song believed to be from the fifteenth century)[9] French *boutarge*, in 1534; Spanish *botarga*, 1580-1590; English botargo, in 1598..." The dates for the word's incursion into Spanish correspond to those which mark the apogee of the *commedia dell'arte* in that country. The *Dizionario etimologico* offers a medieval Latin base—*butarigus* —and suggests its incorporation into Venetian dialect as dating to 1320, much earlier than it appears in other Italian dialects, thereby intensifying the Venice/Pantalone/Bottarga connection. That an Italian actor who played a Venetian merchant-type should take on the name "Bottarga" suggests that the word was clearly associated with that city and its food and that the audience would have recognized it as such.[10] Whether "bottarga" had accrued any humorous and possibly sexual connotation by the end of the sixteenth century (a possible allusion to the prominent phallus normally associated with Pantalone) and if so, whether it was comprehensible to a Spanish audience, I am unable to verify from the texts on hand. I believe we may tentatively assume that the association was not beyond the perception of the spectator given the nature of the mask and of *commedia dell'arte* humor in general (Gordon, *Lazzi* 4).

Lope's repeated presence at the Italian performances (Tomillo 41-42), the numerous references in his plays to Ganassa, Trastullo, Arlecchino and Franceschina (Arco y Garay 721-22) and the imitation of their speech in several plays (Arce 14-15) has been well documented. While the servant masks are those most often recalled by name, Lope seems to have had a per-

---

[9] The reference is to the "Canto della Buttargre" of Piero Cimatore contained in *Tutti i triomphi, carri, mascherate o canti Carnascialeschi andati per Firenze dal tempo del Magnifico Lorenzo vecchio de Medici per infino a questo anno presente 1559* raccolti per Grazzino detto il Lasca, Firenze 1559, as cited by Goulard 199 n. 12.

[10] The practice of associating names with food was common. Among the names given the zanni are "Zan Farina" (Johnny Flour), "Zan Fritata" (Johnny Omelet), "Zan Salcizza" (Johnny Sausage). For other such names see Lea 2:488-94.

46

sonal predilection for that of Pantalone's double, Stefanello Bottarga. During the carnival festivities in Valencia in 1599, Lope appears "costumed allegorically as *Carnival* wearing a *botarga*, an Italian habit which was all red, with breeches and doublet to match, and a long black robe, with a flat black velvet cap on his head... Then the poet Lope de Vega who was dressed as the mask of Estenfanelo Botarga...spoke to his majesty...and said marvelous things in Italian verse like a '*botarga*' which is an Italian figure" (F. de Gauna, 176-77).

Since neither Pantalone nor Stefanello Bottarga is ever mentioned directly by name in Lope's theater, allusions to the mask have to be sought somewhat differently. The incidental use of the word *botarga*, usually in stage directions for comic sequences, refers most often to Pantalone's close-fitting red suit of clothes. In *La boda entre dos maridos* (1595-1601), Pinabel, a lackey attends the university with his master, is stripped down to his underwear by two servants whom he had duped earlier. The stage directions read "Quítenle la sotana y queda en un *botargo* gracioso" 'They take off his tunic and he is left wearing a charming *botarga* (57lb). Stage cues for *El verdadero amante* (1588-95) read "Suena grito que viene un toro; vanse las pastoras, y juegan los pastores con él, y derriba al padrino, que ha de estar vestido de botarga" 'There is a shout that a bull approaches, the shepherdess runs off, the shepherds play with him, and he (the bull) knocks down the friend who is dressed as a *botarga*' (p. 10). In *Las cortes de la muerte*, Folly is a ridiculous, grotesque figure "vestida de botarga, moharracho" 'dressed as a *botarga*' (Shergold, "Ganassa" 366).

The use of the term *botarga* in *Las ferias de Madrid* (1585-88), on the other hand, represents more than a casual reference to Pantalone's or Bottarga's garb. It is tied to the play's comic framework and to its unusual resolution of the honor conflict. The setting for *Las ferias de Madrid* is the festival of St. Matthew replete with rambunctious, pleasure-seeking celebrants. Here an offended husband (Patricio), who learns of his wife Violante's intended infidelity by gaining the confidence of the prospective lover throughout a subterfuge, ends up being killed by his own father-in-law (Belardo) whom he insults for not keeping his word to murder his wayward daughter. (Belardo had asked that he be the one to kill his daughter once she is caught with her lover, a task which in the end he is not up to performing.) The conclusion of the play, clearly antiheroic, makes a travesty of the honor code.[11]

---

[11]   On the burlesque treatment of honor in *Las ferias de Madrid* see Donald McGrady; and Zuckerman-Ingber. I am grateful to Donald McGrady for his analysis of

A close look at the non-narrative elements, i.e. the theatricality of the piece, suggests that what we have here is the conscious reproduction of a *commedia dell'arte* farce. Edwin Morby may have intuited this when he called *Las ferias de Madrid* "a neglected play with *immediatezza rappresentativa* to spare" (297). To date no one has connected the *immediatezza rappresentativa* to the *comici dell'arte*, nor its unusual resolution to the mask of Pantalone. An episode from Act III points the way. The stage directions for a scene in which four gallants go off to a party reads as follows "...entran Roberto, Claudio, y Adrian y Lucrecio vestidos de indio, y de moro, y de pastor y de *botarga* (619b). (The order of the names does not correspond to the costumes; Adrian is the *botarga*.) A fellow reveler accuses Adrian of having dressed as a *botarga* in order to call attention to his body with a clinging suit of clothes. Adrián also wears a sign which recalls the elderly Pantalone's approach to love "Lo que en el gusto amoroso/mi dama no satisfago,/con las galas se la pago" 'what I cannot give in amorous pleasure/I will make up for with gifts' (620a). The sign refers not only to the rich, aged husband of the woman Adrián loves but also the host at a wedding he plans to crash that day. The groom is, once more, a wealthy old man who is marrying a very young girl (622b).

Beyond these allusions to Pantalone, the risible husband destined to be cuckolded, the play abounds in the trickery, pranks and deceptions usually associated with the *commedia dell arte*. Young revelers steal rings from a peddler (587b) and a mirror from a prostitute (597a). They run off without paying after eating their fill (606a) and make off with mutton and fowl belonging to a procuress (614b) [McGrady 37].Youthfull merrymakers beat hapless peasants (589a,b),[12] a servant empties a chamber pot on a gallant's head (589a)[13] and the dialogue is liberally sprinkled with coarse language and clearly sexual *double-entendres* (McGrady 38). Lastly, Lope offers us a heroine who, after exchanging flowery amenities with a young man she has

---

the comic elements which suggested to me the possibility of an extra-literary source. On the Italian novelistic source for *Las ferias de Madrid* (Gian Francesco Straparola's *Le Piacevoli Notti*, IV, 4) see Bruerton 63. For elements taken from the Spanish novelistic tradition (Licentiate Tamariz's *Novela de un estudiante y una dama)* see McGrady, "The burlesque treatment" 39-40.

[12] Twenty-three *lazzi* of violence and sadistic behavior are recorded by Gordon, *Lazzi* 14-19.

[13] Gordon, *Lazzi* 32 lists a "*Lazzo* of the Chamber Pot (Bavaria 1568). The servant-girl (or Franceschina) empties a chamber pot out the window. It hits Pantalone (or the Captain) as he serenades Isabella."

just met, discusses the concrete dangers of love with reference to *orina* (591b).[14]

As concerns the unorthodox ending, I would posit that it may stem not so much from a preconceived stance (i.e. the deliberate ridiculing of the honor code) but from Lope's youthful exhuberance as a dramatist. In his attempt to create a Spanish farce in the style of the *comici* it is not unlikely that Lope may have become caught up in the excitement of the piece and unable to extricate himself, opted for an ending as unexpected as most *lazzi*. It is also conceivable that Lope modeled his play after a comedy he had seen the Italians perform. In the mode of the *commedia dell'arte*, the play has a single intrigue and requires only the simplest of stage sets: a street in front of Violante's home, a plaza and a room for indoor scenes (Bruerton 68). Unfortunately, the *scenari* of the companies performing in Spain have not survived and no extant *scenario* of which I am aware ends with the cuckolded husband being killed by his father-in-law. However, lazzi of violence (beatings, especially of servants) were commonplace. The repertory of Basillio Locatelli contains a "lazzo of killing" in which Zanni and Burattino demonstrate to each other how each would kill Pantalone (or the Captain).Saying "You be Pantalone", Zanni begins to strangle Burattino. With his last breath Burattino says, No, you be Pantalone," an begins to beat Zanni. They continue in tadem (Gordon, *Lazzi* 14). The execution, of course, is never carried out. Perhaps Lope, under pressure to finish the work for a local acting troupe, reported to a turnabout suggested by the players and carried it one step further. Like Pantalone, who must in the end retract hi objections to young love, so Belardo (Lope ?)[15] prepares the way for a similar outcome through an original, last-minute twist of honor ethics. The honor code placed marital fidelity above love and demanded the blood of the offending or intending to offend lovers; the *commedia dell'arte* gave primacy to love.

Reminiscences of Pantalone in Lope's theater, however, are not to be sought exclusively in plays in which the word *botarga* appears textually. A case in point is *La francesilla* (1596).[16] Here, while there is no concrete men-

---

[14]   For the documentation of comic routines concerning urine see Petraccone 263 "Lazzo dell orina" and Gordon, "Sexual/Scatalogical *Lazzi*" in *Lazzi* 32-35.

[15]   That Belardo should be Lope's most common pseudonym (one which he used throughout his lifetime) suggests an even more complex relationship. Was Lope intervening in his own play at the last minute masquerading as Pantalone who, alternately furious yet loving, weeping yet pragmatic, must bring the play to a happy ending? On Lope's use of the pseudonym Belardo in more than sixty plays, see Morley *Pseudonyms* 429-434.

[16]   All verse references to *La francesilla* are taken from the critical edition by

tion of the mask or its garb, the characterization of the father, Alberto, is so clearly molded to Italian specifications as to be immediately recognizable—as it must have been to the contemporary spectator who generally frequented the performances of the *comici* as often as those of his countrymen (Arróniz 216). A brief summary of plot will afford a backdrop against which to measure Lope's delineation of Alberto.

La francesilla recounts the story of Feliciano and Clavelia ("a francesilla") who meet and fall in love in Lyon, France, as Feliciano, accompanied by his servant Tristán, is on his way to fight in Italy. (Feliciano has been sent to war by his father, Alberto, as a disciplinary measure to curb his gambling and womanizing.) Separated from Clavelia by his obligations and by a lovers's misunderstanding, the two are reunited when Clavelia, disguised as a lackey, helps Feliciano escape her brother Teodoro's wrath. (Teodoro had learned of their tryst earlier that evening in a conversation with Feliciano at a nearby inn. Clavelia's subsequent disappearance—she is also running from an unwelcome betrothal to Otavio—sends both men in pursuit of the couple.

Act III (one year later) brings Teodoro and Otavio, posing as French pilgrims, to Madrid. Quite accidentally they are befriended by Alberto and invited to his home. Once aware that Alberto is the father of the man he seeks, Teodoro sets out to avenge the loss of his sister (he believes her dead) through Leonida, Feliciano's sister. Feigning love at first sight, Teodoro asks for her hand. Alberto, impressed by Teodoro's purported wealth, readily accedes.

Shortly thereafter, Feliciano returns to Madrid with Tristan an Clavelia, the latter still in disguise as "Perote" a lackey. There follow a series of lively incidents designed to add to the plot's confusion. Liseno, rejected by Alberto as a suitor for Leonida in favor of the rich Frenchman, succeeds in having Teodoro and Otavio arrested on false charges. Feliciano, unaware that they mean to kill him, arranges for their release. Clavelia's disguise, meanwhile, produces all manner of equivocation. All is forgiven when Feliciano asks Clavelia to appear as herself an the couple is officially betrothed. Teodoro now accepts Leonida's hand in genuine affection and Otavio is promised the hand of Alberto's niece, along with a large dowry. Tristán will marry the maid, Julia.

Donald McGrady, based on the Ignacio Gálvez manuscript transcription of 1762. The Gálvez copy which concretizes the date of the play's completion as April 6, 1596, contains 284 additional verses (McGrady 58). Of these, verses 49-52 were instrumental to the evolution of this study.

That Lope intended to offer his audience a Spanish Pantalone is clear from the outset. Alberto, like Pantalone, opens the play. In the initial dialogue Liseno challenges Alberto's angry reaction to Feliciano's youthful irresponsibility by pointing to Alberto's own vice—his inordinate love of money:

> Tú que el dinero idolatras
> seguiras tu inclinación
> de codicia y ambición
> en usuras y mohatras. (vv. 49-52)

Alberto, as greedy and ambitious as Pantalone, is not above usury and stock manipulation. Like his Italian predecessor, Alberto's unpredictably violent nature is evidenced in the sudden decision to send Feliciano off to war. Liseno's response to the plan as "locura" ('madness') cues the spectator to the tone of Alberto's characterization. Nor can Alberto resist the lure of even greater wealth when Teodoro (Act III), in exchange for Leonida's hand, offers thirty thousand ducats in jewels and ten thousand ducats to be inherited later along with large land holdings. Although Alberto's shrewd business sense motivates him to seek confirmation of Teodoro's riches, Lope underlines Alberto's avarice by contrasting the father's gleeful acceptance to Liseno's angry aside condemning the man's overriding greed.

Alberto's (and Pantalone's) second weakness, even greater than his love of money, is his lascivious streak. Lope gives it ample rein in Act III. Alberto suspects from the beginning that "Perote" is really a young woman and engages the "lackey" in some suggestive repartee (vv. 2564-2572). Sometime later, when he learns from Julia that the "lackey" has been seen hugging Leonida, Alberto flies into a rage, curses his daughter (¡Oh, bastarda!) and sets out to kill "Perote" (vv. 2834-2837). The latter is forced to assuage Alberto's anger with explicit sexual revelations: "Mira que soy caponcillo" "Look, I'm castrated" to which the intervening Tristán adds, "Sí señor, de ambos lados" 'Yes, sir, on both sides'. When Alberto, insisting on proof, demands that Tristan undress "Perote" on the spot (vv. 2874-2879) Tristán is forced to whisper that the lackey is indeed a woman, as Alberto has suspected. Overcome by desire, Alberto now wants to possess Clavelia at any cost, and immediately. He promises Tristán all he owns if he will bring her to his bed that night (vv. 2888-2898). In his blind passion Alberto becomes, like Pantalone, the rival of his own son.

If any doubt remains that Alberto represents a deliberate calque of the Italian prototype, let us consider briefly the context in which the character

51

evolves. *La francesilla* teems with the same representational energy that lay at the heart of the *commedia dell'arte's* success. The Spanish play's vitality is unflagging as Lope heaps intrigue upon intrigue, character upon character, until the plot seems to bursting at the seams. There are no less than nine love triangles. Three of these are created by Clavelia's disguise as "Perote". Julia and Leonida's attraction to "Perote" adds the suggestion of lesbianism to the merriment. The comedy's dynamism is sustained by the lack of reflective moments. Following the Italian pattern, almost all characters are introduced in pairs so that the banter never wanes. The play reverberates with a healthy, sensual zest for life which moves the young lovers to throw caution to the wind. In *commedia dell'arte* performances, order is restored only at the very last moment through Pantalone's forgiveness and the ensuing multiple weddings. *La francesilla* ends with not one, but four couples joined in matrimony, all with Alberto's blessings "Ya todo esta perdonado" 'All is forgiven' (v. 3075).

In the delineation of Alberto Lope captures successfully the contradictory postures which characterize the Italian model. Alberto is greedy yet spontaneously hospitable to the French "pilgrims"; morally indignant over Feliciano's womanizing yet ready to cast aside the stance when "*la francesilla*" catches his fancy; concerned for his daughter's happiness yet not above marrying her off to the highest bidder. Neither Pantalone's nor Alberto's basically serious role as a father precludes his being ridiculed for the less-than-exemplary execution of his duties. Just as the *comici* meant us to laugh at Pantalone, Lope means us to laugh at the mask's Spanish double, Alberto.

The masks, as a group and individually, left an indisputable mark on Lope's theater. As Lope acquired a greater command of his craft, the recollection subsided but never disappeared entirely.[17] In the earlier plays, however, the reminiscences are too patent to be ignored. The absorption and recasting of Pantalone is but one example. That *La francesilla*,[18] as well as *Las ferias de Madrid*, should have its roots in the Italian novelistic tradition, as did a good part of the *commedia dell'arte* repertory either directly or through

---

[17]   Lope paid homage to the acting talents of the *comici* even in his last works. For reference to the famous *prima donna*, Isabella Andreini, in *El castigo sin venganza* (1631) see D'Antuono, *Boccaccio's Novelle* 146-47. Donald McGrady graciously brought to my attention a second encomium to Isabella Andreini in Lope's last play, *Las bizarrías de Belisa*, dated 1634, the year before Lope s death.

[18]   For the Italian novelistic sources of *La francesilla* see McGrady, *La francesilla* 50-56.

earlier stage versions, points to an interrelationship far more complex than has been considered heretofore, and one that warrants further investigation.

Saint Mary's College, Notre Dame

WORKS CITED

Ancona, Allesandro d'. *Origini del* teatro italiano. Torino: Loescher, 1891.

Apollonio, Mario. *Storia del teatro italiano.* Firenze: Sansoni, 1951.

Arce, Joaquin. "Italiano e italianismi cinque-secenteschi in Lope de Vega." *Il Rinascimento. Aspetti e problemi attuali.* Firenze: Olschki, 1982.

Arróniz, Othon. *La influencia italiana en el nacimiento de la comedia española.* Madrid: Gredos, 1969.

Baschet, Armand. *Les Comediens italiens a la cour de France.* Paris: E. Plon, 1882.

Battaglia, Salvatore. ed. *Grande dizionario della lingua italiana.* 3 vols. Torino: Unione Tipografico-Editrice Torinese, 1961.

Bruerton, Courtney. "*Las ferias de Madrid* de Lope de Vega." *Bulletin Hispanique* 57 (1955): 67-69.

Caro Baroja, Julio. "A caza de botargas." *Revista de Dialectología y Tradiciones Populares* 21 (1965): 273-92.

Cotarelo y Mori, Emilio. "Noticias biográficas de Alberto Ganassa." *Revista de Archivos, Bibliotecas y Museos* 19 (1908): 42-61.

Corominas, Joan. *Diccionario crítico etimológico de la lengua castellana.* 3 vols. Berba: Francke, 1954.

Covarrubias Orozco, Sebastian de. *Tesoro de la lengua castellana o española.* Madrid: 1611. Rpt. Barcelona: Horta, 1943. Martín de Riquer, ed.

Diccionario de Autoridades. 1716. Facsimile edition. Madrid: Gredos, 1964.

D'Antuono, Nancy L. "Lope de Vega y la *commedia dell'arte:* Temas y figuras." *Cuadernos de Filología.* Universidad de Valencia 3 (1981): 261-278.

_____. *Boccaccio's "Novelle" in the Theater of Lope de Vega.* Madrid: Porrua Turanzas, 1983. 124-149.

Diaz de Escobar, N. "Anales del teatro español correspondientes a los años 1581-1599." *La Ciudad de Dios.* 82 (1910): 432-440; 789-796; 93 (1971): 146-156.

Falconieri, John V. "Historia de la *commedia dell arte* en España." *Revista de Literatura* 11 (1957): 3-37; 12 (1957): 69-90.

Falconieri, John V. "Mas noticias biográficas de Alberto Ganassa." *Revista de Archi-vos, Bibliotecas y Museos* 60 (1954): 219-222.

García Sanz, S. "Botargas y enmascarados alcarreños." *Revista de Dialectología y Tradiciones Populares* 9 (1953): 466-492.

Garfein, Herschel., and Mel Gordon. "The Adriani *Lazzi* of the Commedia dell'Arte." *Drama Review* 22 (1978): 1-11.

Gauna, F. de. *Libro...del Casamiento y bodas de...Phelipe tercero...*fol. 142. Ed. J. Arreres y Zacarés. Valencia: Imprenta Hijo de F. Vives Mora, 1926.

Gordon, Mel. *Lazzi: The Comic Routines of the Commedia dell'Arte.* Performing Arts Resources, 7. New York: Theater Library Association, 1981.

Goulard, Matilde. "Botarga. Un recuerdo de la comedia italiana." *Mélange de Philolo-gie romane offerts à M. Karl Michäelson.* Goteberg: n. p. 1952. 198-216.

Julia' Martinez, Eduardo. "Lope de Vega en Valencia en 1599." *Boletín de la Real Academia Española* 3 (1916): 541-559.

Lea, Katherine M. *Italian Popular Comedy.* 1934. New York: Russell and Russell, 1962.

Listerman, Randall W. "Some Material Contributions of the *Commedia dell'Arte* to Spanish Theater." *Romance Notes* 17 (1976): 94-198.

_____. La commedia dell'arte: Fuente técnica y artistíca en la dramaturgía de Lope de Rueda." *Actas del Sexto Congreso Internacional de Hispanistas.* Toronto: University of Toronto p., 1980. 64-466.

McGrady, Donald. "The Comic Treatment of Conjugal Honor in Lope's *Las ferias de Madrid.*" *Hispanic Review* 41 (1973): 33-42.

Moliner, Maria. ed. *Diccionario del uso del español.* Madrid: Gredos, 1966.

Morby, Edwin 5. Rev. of *Il teatro valenzano e l'origine della commedia barocca* by Rinaldo Froldi. *Hispanic Review* 32 (1964): 265-268.

Morley, S. Griswold. The Pseudonyms and Literary Disguises of Lope de Vega. Uni-versity of California Publications in Modern Philology 33:5. Berkeley: UP, 1951.

Nicoll, Allardyce. *The World of Harlequin.* Cambridge: Cambridge UP, 1963.

Oreglia, Giacomo. *La Commedia dell'Arte.* Trans. L.F. Edwards. New York: Hill and Wang, 1968.

Pandolfi, Vito. *La Commedia dell'arte. Storia e testo.* Firenze: Sansoni, 1957. 6 vols. 1957-60.

Pellicer, Casiano. *Tratado histórico sobre el origen y progresos de la comedia y del histrionismo en España.* Madrid: Real Arbitrio de Beneficencia, 1804.

Petraccone, E. La commedia dell'arte: storia, tecnica, scenari. Napoli: Ricciardi, 1927.

Place, Edwin D. "Does Lope de Vega's *gracioso* Stem in Part from Harlequin?" *Hispania* 17 (1934): 257-270.

Rasi, V. *I Comici italiani*. Firenze: Francesco Lumachi, 1897.

Rennert, Hugo A. *The Spanish Stage in the Time of Lope de Vega*. New York: Hispanic Society of America, 1909.

Sánchez Arjona, J. *El teatro en Sevilla en los siglos XVI y XVII*. Madrid: A. Alonso, 1887.

Shergold, N.D. "Ganassa and the *Commedia dell.Arte* in Sixteenth-Century Spain." *Modern Language Review* 51 (1956): 359-368.

_____. *A History of the Spanish Stage*. Oxford: Clarendon P., 1967.

Smith, Winifred. *The Commedia dell'Arte. A Study in Italian Popular Comedy* 1912. New York: Benjamin Bloom, 1964.

Tomillo, A. y C. Pérez Pastor. *Proceso de Lope de Vega por libelos contra unos cómicos*. Madrid: Fontanet, Impresor de la Real Academic de la Historia, 1901.

Vega Carpio, Lope Félix. *Amores de Albano y Ismenia. Obras de Lope de Vega*. Nueva edición. Vol 1. Madrid: Real Academia Española, 1918. 13 vols.

_____. *La boda entre dos maridos. Obras de Lope de Vega*. Vol. 14. Madrid: Real Academia Española, 1913. 15 vols. 1890-1913.

_____. *Las ferias de Madrid. Obras de Lope de Vega*. Nueva edicion. Vol. 5. Madrid: Real Academia Española, 1918. 13 vols.

_____. *La francesilla. Obras de Lope de Vega*. Nueva edicion. Vol. 5. Madrid: Real Academia Española, 1918. 13 vols.

_____. *La francesilla*. Ed. Donald McGrady. Charlottesville Virginia: Biblioteca Siglo de Oro, 1981.

_____. *El verdadero amante. Obras de Lope de Vega*. Biblioteca de Autores Españoles 24. Madrid: Atlas, 1945.

Zuckerman-Ingber, Alix. *El bien más alto. A Reconsideration of Lope de Vega's Honor Plays*. Gainesville, Florida: University of Florida Press, 1984.

Fuentes italianas de la mendicidad, la vagancia y el fraude en la novela picaresca española

J. Helí Hernández

Con la publicación del *Lazarillo de Tormes* (1554), se inicia en España un nuevo género literario: la novela picaresca. Por muchos años los estudiosos la consideraron de origen exclusivamente español. Hoy día, sin embargo, la crítica moderna ha rastreado varios de sus elementos temáticos en otras literaturas, especialmente en la italiana.

A partir del Primer Tratado del *Lazarillo*, el episodio del mendigo ciego, en el cual los materiales folklóricos son tan evidentes, alude ya a un tema tradicional en la literatura medieval y renacentista. Así mismo, el episodio del Hidalgo, escudero elegante que mitiga el hambre con el pan que ha mendigado su criado, crea un personaje único de pobre vergonzante. En el Tratado Quinto, el episodio del buldero es un espejo del fraude y del abuso de la credulidad religiosa del pueblo. En la obra maestra del género picaresco, *Guzmán de Alfarache*, Mateo Alemán hace triunfar a su protagonista en los fraudes de los mendigos que explotan la caridad pública. La corporación organizada de mendigos en la cual ingresa y sobresale el pícaro Guzmán se localiza en Roma y es parte de una larga tradición de confraternidades de mendigos. La mendicidad y sobre todo la vagancia y el engaño son aspectos fundamentales de la vida del pícaro, de sus frustaciones y de sus trabajos.

En Europa, la literatura de fines del siglo XV había ya confrontado con atención el fenoneno de la vagancia y sutilmente lo había descrito y analizado. Un manuscrito del *Liber Vagatorum* que circulaba ya a fines del siglo XV, contenía la *Crónica de Basilea* de Johan Knebel, relación manuscrita en la cual se describía el proceso que en 1475 se había efectuado en aquella ciudad contra los vagabundos y los mendigos. Unos años más tarde, entre 1484 y 1486, el *Speculum Cerretanorum*[1] describía un sistema coherente y orgánico de la mendicidad organizada y analizaba sus complicados métodos de fraude. En Europa, contrariamente a cuanto se venía creyendo, el *Speculum Cerretanorum* fue el primer tratado escrito sobre la primogenitura de la literatura de vagabundos y de pícaros. Esta obra, como dice Camporesi: "fa riflettere nella categoria del *"picaresco"*, ritrodatandola e riportandola, almeno in parte, alla matrice medievale. Questi testi costituiscono i remoti incunaboli tardo-medievali della letteratura dei picari e degli straccioni, della *"Lumpenliteratur"* europea, lo specchio straordinario delle astuzie e degli stratagemmi di vagabondi e giuntatori d'ogni risma organizzati nelle loro incredibili confraternite" (XXI-XXII).

El fenómeno de la vagancia reflejaba, sin lugar a duda, la extrema movilidad de una parte de la sociedad medieval, la población errante compuesta de mercantes, vendedores ambulantes, monjes cuestores y vagabundos en fuga del convento; frailes perdonadores o vendedores de reliquias, clerigos sin patria y estudiantes que pedían la caridad. A estas categorías se unía la muchedumbre de peregrinos, auténticos o no, de visionarios, de judíos errantes y de mendigos verdaderos y falsos; de cogregaciones de ciegos y de soldados que iban o venían de las guerras, y de siervos fugitivos que si eran cogidos, en Inglaterra se les marcaba en la frente con una F para indicar "falsedad." Todos ellos eran auténticos desocupados, hambrientos y sin trabajo.

A partir de los primeros años del siglo XV aparecen en la escena otros grupos de vagabundos como los gitanos, los artesanos de temporadas, los albañiles y los trabajadores ambulantes que abandonaban sus pueblos para ejercer su oficio en otras tierras en temporadas breves o largas.[2] Todos ellos llevaban sus vestidos regionales típicos, tenían su propio lenguaje o jerga e iban por el mundo recitando cantilenas y salmodias, convirtiéndose de esta manera en perpetuos vagabundos.

Entre todos los vagabundos sobresale la figura del fraile hipócrita, astuto

---

[1]   El *Speculum Cerretanorum* fue descubierto por Piero Camporesi y lo publicó junto con *Il vagabondo* de Rafael Frianoro bajo el título de *Il libro dei vagabondi*. Según Camporesi, la obra de Frianoro es una mera traducción de la obra de Teseo Pini.

[2]   Inclusive en los postreros años del siglo XVI, Montaigne observaba que a Roma seguían llegando campesinos de todas las regiones de Italia para ganar su sustento durante la temporada de trabajo. Consúltese su *Viaggio in Italia*.

disimulador y pérfido recogedor de limosnas. Como lo describe la literatura tradicional medieval, él es el maestro de todos los mendigos que se burlan de las leyes divinas y humanas:

Ancor si non comanda la scrittura
che possent'uom di corpo cheggia pane,
né che metta a viver d'altru'ane:
questo non piace a Dio né non n'ha cura;
    ne non vuol cbe l'uon faccia sale o mura,
    de le limosine, alle genti strane;
    ma vuol ch'uon le diparta a gente umane
    di cui forza e santade ha gran paura.
E sí difendea "l buono Giustiziano,
e questo fece scriver nella lege,
che nessun dia linosina a uom sano
    che truovi a guadagnare, e tu t'avvegge
    ch'a lavorare e' non vuol metter mano;
    ma vuol che tu 'l gastighi e cacci e fegge. (*Il Fiore, CX*)

En otro soneto de *Il Fiore*, mientras se confronta a un usurero rico y enfermo, es evidente el disgusto y el enojo a la vista de verdaderos mendigos, andrajosos, hambrientos y lacerados:

E quand'io veggo ignudi que' truanti
su' monti del litame star tremando,
che freddo e fame gli va sí accorando
che non posson pregiar né Die né Santi,
    el piu ch'i' posso lor fuggo davanti,
    senza girne nessun riconfortando;
    anzi lor dico: "Al diavol v'accomando
    con tutti que' che non han de' bisanti" (CVII).

El autor de *Il Fiore* muestra aquí uno de los aspectos mas angustiosos de la psicología medieval y una de las contradicciones más agudas de la sociedad cristiana: el amor-odio hacia el pobre; la desgarradora ambigüedad de sentimientos que por una parte identifican al pobre con Cristo, y por otra, lo rechazan con horror como si fuera un paria y un criminal, hasta el punto de hacerlo parte de la familia del diablo en vez de la familia de Cristo, porque "uom ch'é truante col diavol s'afferra" (CXII).[3]

Los grupos de errantes forzados a la vagancia debido a las guerras, a las imposiciones y al hambre se hacían cada vez más numerosos porque la sociedad del tardo medievo arrojaba a las calles al componente más débil de su sociedad. Junto a los errantes profesionales se encontraban también nuevos grupos de "truanti" o vagabundos. El número de los excluídos de la sociedad aumentaba rápidamente con los heréticos, los judíos, los hechiceros y con los enfermos extranjeros que entraban a formar parte de la familia de vagabundos. De esta manera se fomentaron y se e structuraron corporaciones y organizaciones las cuales incluían a toda clase de vagabundos. En Francia, por ejemplo, nació la monarquía del "argot" gobernada por el "Gran Cesare" o "re di Tune" es decir, el rey de la limosna. Este recorría las calles de París en una carreta arrastrada por perros, convirtiéndose así en un símbolo viviente de la antisociedad. En Italia abundaban las sectas y confraternidades de astutos "Cerretani" y las sectas o Abazie dei ribaldi. Especialmente en Toscana triunfó el "Re dei ribaldi" y en Bologna sobresalió la llamada Podestería Marrocorum.[4] Todas estas organizaciones tienen sus imitadores en España en las varias organizaciones de la germanía, fielmente documentada por Cervantes en Rinconete y Cortadillo, y por varios autores de las novelas picarescas.

El problema de la vagancia se incrementaba y se hacía más complicado con los grupos errantes de gitanos que se confudían con otras formas de pobreza y mendicidad cuyo origen, según Polidoro Virgilio, se encontraba en los sacerdotes cuestores de la diosa Siria. Estos sacerdotes cuyo oficio era el pedir limosnas, eran llamados por los italianos "Cilicii." Segun Pietro Valeriano se les llamaba también "Cingani" (259), y según Felipe Canerario, "Ciani" o "Cingari" (Centuria Prima, 95-96). El fraude y el engaño, afirma Polidoro, había empezado con los sacerdotes de la diosa Siria y después se había ramificado a las clases más bajas de la sociedad y posteriormente se había difundido por todas las tierras habitadas. Al identificar una fuente remota del arte del engaño, Polidoro lo explica haciendo responsables a los "Cilicii", es decir, a los gitanos.

Después de analizar detalladamente la organización de los gitanos,

---

[3] El vocablo "truante" parece haber pasado a la lengua italiana del término francés "truand", convirtiéndose en un sinonimo más para indicar "accatone", "mendicante" y "vagabondo."

[4] En Italia, los estafadores o engañadores eran llamados "Marocchi" o "baratti." Vease L. Frati, La vita privata in Bologna dal secolo XIII al XVII.

Piero Camporesi cree improbable que ellos hayan aportado a los vagabundos europeos, ya sea los métodos de organizacion, sus técnicas o su lengua. De hecho, los gitanos no sólo aparecen en grupo en la escena europea en una época mas bien reciente — en Alemania alrededor del 1417, en Italia en la tercera década del siglo XV y en España en 1447 — sino que sea el *Speculum* como el *Liber Vagatorum* demuestran que ya en el siglo XV las artes del disfraz y del engaño estaban fuertemente organizadas según el espíritu social del mundo europeo. Estas dos obras delinean una sociedad que se desarrolla según esquemas profundamente intrínsecos y que no tenían necesidad de buscar en el nomadismo de origen oriental, modelos de desarrollo o técnicas de perfeccionamiento.[5]

De mucha mas importancia en el desarrollo de la vagancia son los grupos y las bandas de falsos peregrinos que pululaban por todas partes y con estratagemas y amenazas obtenían hospitalidad, dinero y vestidos. Todos estos peregrinos iban protegidos por una aureola misteriosa de devoción. Decían que iban a Loreto o a Roma, a Jerusalem, a Santiago de Compostela[6] y de esta manera suscitaban en la gente que los escuchaba maravilla, caridad y muchas veces envidia. En tiempos de devoción, mucha gente decidía hacerse peregrinos y viajaba a los santuarios más famosos sin importarle la distancia. Los que acogían y hospedaban decidían hacerse peregrinos, contagiados por el deseo de emulación y se sentían empujados a hacer otro tanto. Todos veían en el forastero o peregrino la encarnación de un deseo latente de viajes y aventuras por las vías que conducían a la remisión de los pecados. La Virgen de los peregrinos protegía a los romeros; los santos los guiaban y la caridad de los hombres proveía a su sustento. La astucia y el engaño eran, sin embargo, los mejores medios de su subsistencia

---

 [5]   En la introducción a *Il libro dei vagabondi,* Piero Camporesi rechaza la tesis de Henry Kamen de que el problema de la vagancia haya sido solamente un problema de gitanos, Así mismo rechaza la afirmación de que la organización de los mendigos seguía los modelos que el nomadismo gitano proponía a los vagabundos de occidente. En cuanto al lenguaje, Camporesi demuestra que existe una marcada diferencia entre la jerga de los gitanos y la de los vagabundos, como lo comprueba el *Speculum.* (XXXVI)
 [6]   En la continuación del *Guzmán de Alfarache* de Félix Machado de Silva, en un momento de peligro, el pícaro protagonista hace el voto de una peregrinación: "dixe que era forzoso partirme el siguiente día a Santiago de Galizia, vestido de peregrino, por voto que un peligro grande, de que el me sacara avía hecho," Véase "*Tercera parte de Guzmán de Alfarache,*" ed, Gerhard Moldenhawer. Conviene recordar que la vida vagabunda del pícaro ha sido interpretada como una dolorosa peregrinación dentro del concepto católico romano de la peregrinación de la vida. Consultese al respecto Juergen Hahn, *The Origins of the Baroque Concept of Peregrinatio.*

como lo demuestra la *Canzone di pellegrini truffatori*: "in ogni loco, ogni clima, ogni parte/ e "l viver nostro archimia, astuzia e arte" (Camporesi XXXVIII).

Muchos de los falsos peregrinos pasaron su vida vagando por el mundo y se hacían pasar por magos y brujos:

> Pieno e il mondo di falsi profeti
> d'astrologhi sibille e di resie
> di sogni e fantasie,
> d'indovini d'auguri e negromanti. (Sacchetti, *Il libro*, 254)

Junto a estos peregrinos se encontraba tambien otra clase de vagabundos los cuales quedaban satisfechos cuando recibían algo de dinero para gastarlo en la taberna. Estos eran los llamados *"lanzi pellegrini"* que pedían limosnas en nombre de la "Caritate amore Dei." Los *"lanzi"* formaban una serie de grupos, tantos cuantos eran los oficios que dependían de las estaciones, de los viajes y de las andanzas. En la lengua italiana de los siglos XV y XVI, sus nombres evocaban imágenes de hombres consagrados a oficios vagabundos, inestables y ambulantes. Los *"lanzi"* eran *"maestri sonatori di ribecchini"*, *"tagliatori a tavola"*, *"coltellinai"*, *"cozzoni"* y *"venturieri."* Estos artesanos errantes, vagabundos por necesidad o por vocación, cuando se encontraban en dificultad, se hacían pasar por peregrinos:

> Misericordie e caritate
> alle pofer Lancresine
> che l'argente pel cammine
> tutt'ha spese e consumate... (*Nuovi Canti...* 19)

Entre los *"lanzi"* existían también confraternidades de *"storpiati"* que con monótonos lamentos movian a la caridad:

> Qeste qui profer taucce
> ha un triste gamberucce,
> zoppe, zoppe va con grucce
> e rattratte star d'un braccie:
> foller lui qualche cenciaccie
> da facciar suo moncherine, (*Nuovi Canti...* 116)

Otro grupo era el de los *"lanzi romiti"*, que iban vendiendo falsas reliquias:

61

Questi tanti catriossi
tutte star reliquie sante;
chi afer diavoli addossi
star cazzar vie tutte quante,
non per forze o false incante
ma per lor divin potenze, (*Nuovi Canti*... 54)

Muchos de estos grupos, sin embargo, se originaban, se transformaban y rápidamente desaparecían. Durante su efímera existencia, todos ellos vivían de la caridad de la gente que de buen o de mal grado los mantenía ya que pedían en nombre de Cristo o de los Santos.

Junto a estos grupos o sectas que mendigaban, a veces dentro del límite de la ley y otras fuera de ella, existían también grupos originalmente reconocidos por la Iglesia, pero que con el pasar del tiempo, habían exagerado los derechos de su labor y andaban sembrando errores. Entre estos grupos sobresalen los cuestores que, mientras se dirigían a Roma, pedían limosnas para los lugares santos de Oriente. Los cuestores predicaban públicamente, conmovian a los curiosos y prometiendo indulgencias o amenazando con la excomunión, obtenían las limosnas y el dinero que buscaban. El hecho de que la gente les creyese se explica debido al clima psicológico de aquellos tiempos y al sentimiento popular que prevalecía. Era una época de idolatría católica y de fe ciega en los milagros y en las reliquias de los Santos. Aún más, existía un comercio escandaloso de huesos de Santos y de reliquias de la cruz. Era ésa una época de supersticiones sin límite, de peregrinaciones faltas de un verdadero espíritu religioso y de prácticas religiosas meramente externas. Refiriéndose a las creencias religiosas de los italianos, Martín Lutero critica duramente su religiosidad externa:

Grande é la cecitá e la superstizione degl' Italiani, perche per i colpi hanno piú paura di sant'Antonio e di san Sebastiano che di Cristo. Perció se uno vuole conservar pulito un posto, perche non ci si pisci, come fanno gl'Italiani alla maiera dei cani, ci dipinga su un'immagine di sant'Antonio con la punta di legno e questa immagine scaccia quelli che stanno per pisciare. Insomma l'Italia e tutta una superstizione, e gl'Italiani vivono soltanto nelle superstizioni senza la parola, di Dio e senza la predicazione, e cosí non credono né alla resurrezione della carne né alla vita eterna; hanno solo una gran paura delle ferite corporali e delle disgrazie. Perció hanno piu paura di san'Antonio e di san

Sebastiano che di Cristo, che é stato un fratello mansueto e affettuoso, (*Discorsi*, 243).

Las palabras de Martín Lutero sobre la religiosidad de los italianos son fuertes pero substancialmente verdaderas. El, que conocía bien las prácticas religiosas en Alemania, quiso escribir el Prefacio de la edición del *Liber Vagatorum* publicada en Wittenberg en 1528, para censurar no sólo a los vagabundos y falsos mendigos, sino también a los frailes cuestores.

Sorprende quizás la facilidad con la cual los engañadores lograban extorsionar el dinero de la gente. La caridad y la piedad estaban profundamente arraigadas en la religiosidad popular, pero junto a ellas existía también el culto supersticioso a los Santos, las reliquias y la fe ingenua en la fuerza sobrenatural y mágica de cantilenas. Los astutos e impostores vivían una época dorada. En Italia, durante la segunda mitad del siglo XV, todas las categorías de la impostura: falsos cuestores, falsos predicadores, falsificadores de reliquias, falsos peregrinos, falsos enfermos, falsos mendigos, etc, etc., son catalogadas y analizadas por Teseo Pini.[7] Nos encontramos frente a un mundo increíble de engaños, frente a la industria sutil y universal del fraude. Según Teseo Pini, la industria del engaño era la octava de las Artes Liberales y la definía como "*la profonda e nobile arte della furfanteria*", es decir, el arte de la picardía.

Los placeres de esta "*dolce arte*" hará que por las plazas de Italia se entone alegremente la canción del pícaro:

La piú bella arte che sia,
Si é la gagliofferia,
E lo inverno stare al sole,
E la state all'ombria,
E tener la frasca in mano
E la mosca cacciar vía,
E mangiar la carne grassa
E la magra gettar via. (D'Ancona 2, 612)[8]

---

[7] En el *Speculum*, Pini reporta un total de 39 categorías diferentes de fraude y engaño. En la traducción del latín al italiano hecha por Rafaele Frianoro en el siglo XVII, el número de categorías fue reducido a 34.

[8] Ecos de la canción del pícaro italiano son las palabras de Lázaro de Tormes en la continuación o *Segunda Parte* de H. de Luna: "Si he de decir lo que siento, la vida picaresca es vida, que otras no merecen ese nombre; si los ricos la gustasen, dejarían por ella sus haciendas ...... la vida picaresca es más descansada que la de reyes,

Al canto del pícaro italiano se unían también las voces que se alzaban en las tabernas en parodia de lo sagrado: "Ma sopra tutto nel buon vino ho fede/e credo che sia salvo chi gli crede," (*Il Morgante* XVIII 115). La tabernas, de hecho, se habían transformado en sucursales de los conventos y de las sacristías. En ellas, los fraíles perdonadores, los curanderos y charlatanes, y los vendedores de falsas reliquias hacían sus negocios mientras recitaban las Letanías de los buenos compañeros, o mientras decían el Padre Nuestro del vino. En la taberna de Vannosso, conocido vagabundo, se encuentra ya esa atmósfera de perdición:

> Perdoni e cavalieri fative avanti
> e vederete i Santi andar per terza,
> e la fe' che sí sguerza ogni di piú:
> Satán e Belzebú tengon la rocca
> di questa nostra cocca in mar perita,
> zoé de nostra vita,
> senza veruna aita né governo:
> questo é dritto inferno
> con pene in sempiterno e morsi d'anemi,
> ch'han questi pusillamini
> ch'a l'asaro si danno.
> Ciascun va con enganno e pien di zacare
> sonando trombe e nachare al buon Cristo... (*Le rime* 242-243).

Teniendo en cuenta este ambiente general de perdición y de engaño, no debe sorprender que en la segunda mitad del siglo XV, ya sea en Italia como fuera de ella, se hayan escrito obras con una intención común. El *Speculum*, el *Novellino*, el *Liber Vagatorum*, en su manuscrito primitivo, e inclusive los versos de Sebastian Brant contra los mendigos en su obra *Stultifera navis*, denuncian a los engañadores del mundo, especialmente a los fraíles y monjes que "venden" el nombre de Dios para comer y beber. Contra estos "*monachos manducantes, alias mendicantes*," Sacchetti imprecaba:

> Ogni prelato corre
> non a dar, ma a torre
> e non si puote opporre

_____

emperadores y papas." Véase Alborg, I, 753-754.

a la lor legge;
Vendendo Dio, e'templi e le lor segge. (*Il libro...*297)

Por lo que se refiere a frailes y religiosos, el *Novellino* documenta y
abiertamente crítica sus abusos. En la Novela 3 expone la plaga de la
simonía; en las Novelas 3 y 4 critica las conesiones y absoluciones dadas a
cambio de dinero y censura la falsificación de reliquias; y en la Novela 18
desenmascara los frailes de San Antonio, secta reservada casi exclusivamente a los espoletinos y cerretanos, los cuales viajaban por toda Italia predican-
do y fingiendo milagros[9] y después de haber engañado a los crédulos
regresaban a sus casas a la poltronería.

Una galería de falsarios semejante a la descrita por el *Novellino* es la que
presenta Rafael Frianoro en la traducción que hace del *Speculum*. De los
numerosos grupos de falsarios reportados sobresalen los siguientes: a) Los
"*bianti*", llamados también "*pitocchi*', los cuales falsificaban y llevaban consigo bulas pontificias. Estos repartían abundantemente indulgencias y
prometían sacar las almas del purgatorio y con frecuencia se creían con el
poder de rescatar las almas que habían sido condenadas al infierno. b) Los
"*falsi bordoni*" eran aquellos que fingían ser peregrinos y por lo tanto fingían
estar llenos de espíritu divino. c) Los "*affrati*" o falsos frailes eran quellos que
bajo el hábito falso de religiosos cometían toda clase de indignidades y
muchas veces eran tomados por verdaderos religiosos. d) Los "*affarfanti*"
eran verdaderos furfantes pícaros que fingían milagros y decían haber come-
tido graves y enormes pecados. e) Los "*reliquiari*" decían que llevaban consigo las reliquias de los Santos. A pesar de las prohibiciones canónicas de mos-
trar reliquias fuera del relicario y sin la aprobación del Papa, los "*reliquiari*"
llevaban consigo falsas reliquias que mostraban a la gente crédula y con frecuencia las vendían para conseguir dinero. f) Los "*accapponi*" que fingían
tener grandes y temibles plagas en las piernas. Para mover a compasión y
obtener generosas limosnas, los "*accapponi*" usaban la yerba "*aron*" o "*arum
italicum*" que tenía la propiedad de simular úlceras.[10]

El fraude organizado encontraba su fuerza y su estímulo en el profundo
espíritu religioso con raíces en la religiosidad medieval. El mendigo siempre

---

[9] Como repetidamente se ha dicho, el milagro fingido del episodio del
buldero, en el Tratado V del *Lazarillo*, es un ejemplo típico del abuso de las cosas
sagradas y de la fe popular con el propósito de obtener dinero.

[10] El *Arum italicum* era también conocido, en Italia con el nombre de "*erba da
piaghe*." En el *Guzmán de Alfarache*, el protagonista revela las técnicas que se usaban
en aquellos, tiempos para la simulación de las úlceras, Véase *Guzmán*, 1, III, IV.

estuvo rodeado de un respeto sagrado y religioso, ya sea que se le considerase hombre de Dios o que se viese en él al pecador que iba errante para expiar sus culpas. El sentido de religiosidad es un componente vital de la mendicidad y de la vagancia, pero no es el único. Según los observadores de la sociología de la vagancia, el aspecto socio-económico también es de suma importancia.

El problema religioso y socio-económico de la mendicidad surgió en toda su gravedad en el siglo XVI. En España, más quizás que en cualquier otro país europeo, fue donde se discutió y trató de darse una solución al problema de la mendicidad y de los pobres. El anhelo de solución por parte de las autoridaes religiosas y civiles dio origen a una debatida polémica con dos posiciones claramente opuestas, planteadas y defendidas por Luis Vives y Domingo de Soto. Vives fue el portavoz de una austera burguesía, la cual veía la solución al problema de la mendicidad en el trabajo. En su obra, *De Subventione Pauperum* (1526), Vives atacó los abusos de los mendigos proponiendo métodos de recuperación social. Soñó con la rehabilitación de todos los mendigos, incluso los impedidos e inválidos. A pesar de haber sido duramente criticado por Lorenzo de Villavicencio de intentar secularizar la beneficencia, su obra dio como resultado temporal que el poder central de España se sintiera con autoridad para exigir a las ciudades que se hicieran cargo de los pobres. En 1545 en Zamorá, Salamanca y Valladolid se promulgaron ordenanzas para asistir a los pobres en su domicilio o en los hospitales por medio de subscripciones permanentes.

Las tentativas de reforma fracasaron debido a las ideas que Domingo de Soto tenía sobre la mendicidad. En *Causa Pauperum Deliberatio* (1545), De Soto defendió la mendicidad tradicional y los derechos de los mendigos, fueran éstos verdaderos o falsos. Continuando los argumentos de San Juan Crisóstomo, De Soto afirmaba que "in dubio, pro paupere", (*Deliberatio*, IX), No se hacían preguntas para averiguar el verdadero estado del mendigo porque para la gente buena y sobre todo para los religiosos, el mendigo continuaba siendo un hombre de Dios,[11] A pesar de la publicación del *De Sub-*

---

[11]   La anécdota del beato Tomás de Villanueva, Arzobispo de Valencia, revela la sensibilidad hacia los pobres, Se cuenta que estando asomado a su ventana observando la distribución de la limosna, el beato se dio cuenta que un pobre discutía con su ecónomo. Preguntando la razón de la discusión, el ecónomo respondió que aquel pobre, después de haber recibido su parte, trataba, con engaño, de recibir la limosna por segunda vez. A esto respondió el Arzobispo: "no entendeis las cosas de los pobres, dadle la limosna por segunda vez. Quizás sea el mismo Cristo que en forma de este pobre viene a probar nuestra caridad, Dad, dad," Véase Camporesi LXXXI.

ventione, obra considerada como el principio del fin de la vagancia, la mendicidad en España y en Europa tuvo aún momentos de gran esplendor.

Si bien los clérigos y las autoridades religiosas veian a Cristo en el pobre o mendigo, con frecuencia fueron acusadas de negligencia en cuanto a sus deberes cristianos. La voz severa y reprimente de Vives se dirigió sobre todo a las instituciones eclesiásticas degeneradas cuyas acciones eran ineficaces. Vives se quejó especialmente de la negligencia del clero en cuanto a deberes pastorales y también de la falta de acción por parte de las autoridades civiles. La obra de Vives fue, sin lugara duda, el primer intento para resolver el problema de la mendiidad mediante la reeducación de los mendigos y la enseñanza de un oficio para alejarlos de las calles y de la vagancia.

Varias son las obras que siguen a las de Vives y De Soto en a polémica sobre los pobres y mendigos. Entre otras, la de Fray Juan de Medina, *De la orden que en algunos pueblos de España se ha puesto en la limosna, para remedio de los verdaderos pobres.* (1545). Fray Juan llegó a la conclusión de que "el mendigo fingido es ladrón," También la obra de Cristóval Pérez de Herrera, *Discuros del amparo de los legítimos pobres y reducción de los fingidos, de la fundación y principio de los albergues destos Regnos, amparo de la milicia dellos* (1598). En esta obra, Pérez de Herrera presentó a Felipe III un plan para solucionar la mendicidad y que consistía en la reclusión de los mendigos.

Es natural que sea en la España del siglo XVI donde se multiplican los tratados en pro y en contra de los mendigos. Sin lugar a duda, las obras sobre pobres y mendigos son una guía para entender mejor la literatura picaresca y su bajo fondo social como reflejo de una sociedad en profunda crisis. Por los caminos de España menudeaban más de 150.000 vagabundos, mendigos, bandoleros y pícaros de las mas variadas especies, expertos en la tarea de engañar para ganarse la vida. Fernando Braudel afirma que estos vagabundos tenían sus ciudades y sus lugares preferidos. En Sevilla, el Matadero; cerca de Sevilla, San Lucar de Barrameda; y en Madrid, la Puerta del Sol. Entre los vagabundos, los mendigos constituían una confraternidad y con frecuencia se reunían en gran número. Por las calles que conducían a Madrid se encontraban otras categorías de pobres que conmovían los corazones más endurecidos. Eran éstos funcionarios sin oficio, capitanes sin compañía en busca de trabajo y que muriéndose de hambre esperaban que en la capital se decidiese su suerte.

También formaban parte del mundo de la vagancia los soldados, los reclutas y los personajes picarescos que eran contratados para trabajar por temporadas, En 1586, en Valencia, el virrey tomó drásticas medidas contra los desocupados, especialmente contra los vagabundos que en los días de trabajo jugaban en las plazas públicas con el pretexto de que no encontraban trabajo. En realidad, la mayoría de ellos eran ladrones y delincuentes por lo cual el reino estaba preocupado. De igual manera se obró contra los que decían ser mendigos y contra todos los que trataban de vivir sin trabajar.

Medidas análogas a las españolas fueron tomadas también n Italia, En 1590, en Palermo se tomaron medidas represivas contra "i vagabondi, ubriaconi e spioni del regno." (Braudel 873-877). Por otra parte, varios textos literarios de la época corroboran las medidas recriminatorias contra los desocupados. En una Novela de Celio Malespini se lee que en Génova habían desterrado a todos los vagabundos "i quali non potevano dimorare senza licenza" (85). En *Piazza universale*, Tommaso Garsoni atestigua que el Gran Duque Cósimo de Toscana había llenado las galeras de su flota con los vagabundos que andaban dispersos por las ciudades del Estado de su Señoría.

En los postreros años del Renacimiento y en las primeras décadas del Barroco, la ciudad de Roma ofrecía la mejor muestra de la hunamidad mendicante y engañadora. A ella como centro de la cristiandad llegaban muchedumbres de peregrinos, de aventureros, de viajeros y de mendigos verdaderos y falsos. Con las limosnas papales y la munificencia de los Cardenales, Roma era la ciudad soñada por los cristianos de todo el mundo y especialmente por los pícaros. Aunque ya se había terminado la época del Duque Valentino, "protector de los ociosos y vagabundos" (Delicado 347). Roma, sin embargo, era aún una especie de Meca, no sólo para los pícaros de España, sino también para todos los vagabundos de Europa. El paraíso romano de los pícaros descrito en el *Guzmán de Alfarache* no es mera invención literaria. A Roma se dirigían todos los vagabundos y día tras día aumentaba el número de los desocupados y de los mendigos, hasta el punto que a principios del siglo XVII, asevera Camillo Fanucci, "non si vede altro che poveri mendicanti, e in tanto numero, che non si puó stare né andare per le strade che continuamente l'uomo non sia attorniato da questi..." (67). Esta alarmante situación movió a los Papas de la Contrarreforma a grandes obras de caridad que dieron origen al nacimiento de varios hospitales entre los cuales figura el hospital de los "*Pobres Mendicantes*" (1587), construído por voluntad del Papa Sixto V. Muchos de los mendigos, sin embargo, prefirieron la vida libre de la calle a la vida en un hospital y la famosa plaza Navona continuó siendo el lugar favorito de vagabundos y desocupados.

A pesar de las muchas obras de caridad en favor de los mendigos, por estos años se empezaba a respirar también un aire de represión contra ellos.

En 1589, por ejemplo, cierto hombre llamado Marcello, le escribió al Cardenal Antonio Carafa para que tomara medidas severas contra los vagabundos. Marcello documentaba la proliferación de mendigos y vagabundos no sólo con observaciones personales, sino también con un ejemplar manuscrito del *Speculum Cerretanorum*. Por otra parte, en la curia romana existía ya cierta hostilidad contra las viejas organizaciones de cuestores. Las condiciones sociales de la época exigían una revisión y transformación de las confraternidades que habían prosperado en la época medieval. Varios grupos de cuestores romanos, como la *"Compagnia di Santa Elisabetta,"* negociaban con el poder político y con la policía su sobrevivencia a cambio de un impuesto mensual que era destinado a cubrir los gastos de ciertas ceremonias religiosas. Esto significaba que estaban controlados por las autoridades con las cuales colaboraban a cambio de impuestos. Su campo de actividad era conocido, limitado y se comprometían a no cometer otras actividades criminales fuera de su sector. Todas estas hermandades o compañías se especializaban cada vez más en una actividad particular e irónicamente exigían que no se les confundiese con las compañías de ladrones. Sus estatutos excluían a los bribones que se dedicaban a otra clase de trucos que no fueran los establecidos por la hermandad. En las *Ordenanzas Mendicativas* reportadas en el *Guzmán de Alfarache,* la corporación romana de mendigos excluía rigurosamente a todos aquellos que ejercían actividades incompatibles con la ética del mendigo puro.

En conclusión, no sorprende que la mendicidad, la vagancia y el fraude hayan concluido un ciclo en la novela picaresca cuyos personajes son vagabundos, ingeniosos, astutos, aventureros y falsarios de las cosas sagradas y profanas. Lo mismo había sucedido con otros temas, como el de la *"bolsa encontrada"* que en su version italiana incluye a San Bernardino de Siena engañado por dos pícaros. Como de costumbre, el origen se halla en el *Novellino, Novela 16,* reaparece en el *Capítulo VI del Speculum* con los *"falsi bordones"* y termina su trayectoria literaria en el *Guzmán de Alfarache,* II, III, V.

University of Lowell

OBRAS CITADAS

Alborg, Juan Luis. *Historia de la literatura española*, Vol, I. Segunda edición ampliada. Madrid: Gredos, 1972,

Anónimo, *Il Fiore e Il Detto d'amore*. A cura di E. G. Parodi. Firense: Bempotrat, 1932.

_____. *Nuovi canti carnascialeschi del Rinascimento*. A cura di Charles S. Singleton. Modena: Societá tipografica Modenese, 1940.

Braudel, Fernand. *Civiltá e imperi del Mediterraneo nell'etá di Filippo II* Torino: Einaudi, 1953.

Camerario, Filippo. *Operae horarum subcisivarum, sive meditationes historicae, Centuria secunda*. Francofurti, 1958.

Camporesi, Piero. *Il libro dei vagabondi*. Torino: Einaudi, 1973.

Clebert, Jean-Paul. *The Gypsies*. Paris: Les Tziganes, 1961.

D'Ancona, Alessandro. *Origini del teatro italiano*. Torino: Loescher, 1891.

Delicado, Francisco. *Retrato de la loçana andaluza*. Edicíon crítica de Bruno M. Damiani y Giovanni Allegra. Madrid: Porrúa Turanzas, 1975.

Fanucci, Camillo, *Trattato di tutte l'opere pie dell'alma cittá di Roma*. Roma, 1602.

Frati, L. *La vita privata in Bologna dal secolo XIII al XVII*. Bologna: Zanichelli, 1928.

Hahn, Jurgen, *The origins of the Baroque Concept of Peregrinatio*. Chapel Hill: The University of North Carolina Press, 1973.

Kamen, Henry, *The Iron Century Social Change in Counter-Reformation Europe*. London: Weindenfeld and Nicholson, 1971,.

Lutero, Martín. *Discorsi a tavola*. Introduzione, traduzione e note a cura di Leandro Perini. Torino: Einaudi, 1969.

Malespini, Celio. *Novelle scelte*. A cura di Ettore Allodoli, Lanciano: Carabba, 1915.

Montaigne, Michel De. *Viaggio in Italia*, Traduzione di I. Riboni, Milano: Bompiani, 1947.

Sacchetti, Franco, *Il libro delle rime*. Bari: Laterza, 1936

_____. *Il Trecentonovelle*. A cura di E. Faccioli Torino: Einaudi, 1970.

Valeriano, Ioannis Pierii. *Hieroglyphica*. Lugduni: Frelon, 1602.

Vannozzo, Francesco. *Le rime*, A cura di Antonio Medin, Bologna: Commissione per i testi bilingui, 1928.

Captación auditiva e imagen visual en la Roma de Francisco Delicado y Pietro Aretino

Louis Imperiale

Más allá de la similitud temática que existe en todos los niveles entre *La Lozana andaluza* e *I ragionamenti*,[1] nos proponemos enfocar nuestro estudio alrededor de la actitud de cada escritor frente al material lingüístico y literario con el que describe a Roma, espacio literario y escenario teatral por excelencia de las aventuras de Lozana y las de Nanna.

En el relato de Delicado, el lector va descubriendo, paulatinamente, una Roma españolizada al máximo, mientras que Aretino, en su narración, evoca una visión de la Urbe más doméstica (no olvidemos que uno era extranjero y el otro italiano auténtico). El autor andaluz privilegia, en gran medida, la vertiente acústica de esta Roma-Babilonia, capital de la cristian-

---

[1] Véase el paralelismo que establece Bruno Damiani en *Francisco Delicado*, entre Delicado y Aretino, y la nota de Mario Baratto en *Teatro y luchas sociales: Ruzante, Aretino, Goldoni*, que reproducimos a continuacion:
"La originalidad de Aretino no se anula con las obras que hubieran podido ser su base, entre las cuales es importante, puesto que está fundada sobre un cuadro del ambiente romano, *El retrato de la Lozana andaluza* del sacerdote español Francisco Delicado, editado en 1528 en Venecia. Es muy importante la cantidad de temas que confluyen en *I Ragionamenti*: el cuadro costumbrista, el galanteo erótico, la parodia del tratado amoroso especialmente la literatura en torno a las meretrices, abundantísima en aquella época (especialmente en la literatura inventiva, en la cual se había distinguido Lorenzo Veniero ya en el año 1530). . . "(Nota 8, p. 300).
Todas las citas textuales de la obra de Francisco Delicado se tomarán de la edición de Bruno Damiani y Giovanni Allegra, abreviada en LADA, seguida por el número del mamotreto y la página de la cita. Las referencias textuales de la obra de Pietro Aretino serán tomadas de la edición de Giovanni Aquilecchia, *Sei giornate*.

dad sólo en aparencia. En realidad, esta ciudad se había transformado en un centro del juego y del sexo.

A través de sus 125 personajes, el "auctor" de Lozana se familiariza con los mínimos ruidos, sonidos, risas, conversaciones y altercados de las calles, las plazas, las ferias y los establecimientos públicos tales como las "estufas," los garitos, las tabernas y los lupanares. Resulta patente que la pluma de nuestro sacerdote cordobés se interesó menos por el arte "académico" del escritor que por los efectos inmediatos que su texto podía producir en el universo mental del lector-oyente. Este lenguaje hablado parece, como lo observa Stephen Gilman, a propósito de *La Celestina*, "emerger de una vida y dirigirse a otra" (Stephen Gilman, 40).

El poder de Lozana proviene menos de una fuerza física que de un dominio de la palabra y de los medios de persuasión que nuestra andaluza lleva junto con su "canastillo." La comunicación oral es su instrumento de trabajo predilecto. Desde su llegada a Roma, Lozana quiere que los demás la oigan, sabe impresionar a sus compañeras de Pozo Blanco. Con Rampín, la "sin par" toma todas las decisiones. Sin embargo, no monopoliza siempre el tiempo de palabra, sabe escuchar y aprovechar, por ejemplo, los consejos y el "conocimiento" prodigioso del balijero. Con Lozana la novela dialogada se redacta a compás con el ritmo del discurso de nuestra heroína y de los diálogos con los demás personajes. Advertimos un fenómeno muy extraño en esta relación entre Lozana y el "auctor," y es que este último debe subordinarse a los actos y a las etapas de la vida de esta mujer. Este dinámico personaje establece e impone al "auctor" las premisas de unos recursos narrativos que estén en armonía con la realidad romana, en otras palabras, obliga a su creador a rebasar las fronteras del discurso narrativo. Por tal razón, en el mamotreto XIV, una vez que Lozana y Rampín se duermen, después de la escena erótica, el "auctor" se queda despierto y nos dice:

Lozana.—¡Mira qué sueño tiene, que no puede ser mejor! Quiérome yo morir.
Auctor.—Quisiera saber escrivir un par de ronquidos, a los quales despertó él y queriéndola besar, despertó ella, y dixo: — ¡Hay señor! ¿Es de día?
Ranpín.—No sé, que agora desperté, que aquel cardo me ha hecho dormir (LADA XIV, 145)

¿Y por qué? Porque cuando Lozana duerme, el "auctor" se queda "desempleado." Este no puede describir los ronquidos como no puede describir los momentos de silencio. Cualquier músico confesará que lo más difícil de tocar en una partitura musical es un silencio. El silencio es el "enemigo" del oído. El "auctor" proxeneta debe tener a su personaje-prostituta en continuo movimiento y por eso le agrega 124 personajes para que no haya grandes espacios de silencio, por esta razón, cuando los personajes parlanchines silencian, oímos algo muy fuerte, por cierto: el ronquido.

Si el "auctor" va escribiendo los apuntes a medida que ocurren los hechos, la Nanna de Aretino cuenta los hechos "aprés coup." Esta es una de las razones por la que tenemos en *I ragionamenti* una vertiente acústica y otra pictórica en la evocación de la ciudad. Nanna puede suspender la narración para describir los objetos, los lugares y las personas: una celda de convento, unos frescos obscenos, un pedagogo repugnante, un pedazo de terreno del "Monte Calvario." Al narrar su pasado, Nanna tiene un cierto control sobre el tiempo, mientras que Lozana, viviendo sus aventuras a medida que el "auctor" las va apuntando, no puede detener el desarrollo de la acción para deleitarse en una descripción. Por ser un texto "actualizado," Delicado no tiene que privilegiar así lo auditivo. Hubiéramos podido "ver" más cosas a través de los personajes. Es que, entre otras cosas, Delicado se inserta en la línea del texto dialogado de *La Celestina*. Es género establecido. Nanna, en cambio, tuvo veinte años para "ensayar" lo que está narrando.

El autor de Lozana compone su relato a la vez que su heroína vive las aventuras. Nos parece capital entender este fenómeno, porque es una de las diferencias fundamentales en la que estriba la divergencia de puntos de vista del ambiente romano de los dos escritores. El "auctor" de Lozana apunta las palabras tales como salen de la boca de los personajes y estos personajes pertenecen, además, a distintas comunidades sociales y lingüísticas. Por esta razón es casi natural encontrar en el relato de Delicado una lengua franca que es menos obvia en *I ragionamenti* a pesar de que Aretino acepta, como lo señala Francesco De Sanctis en *Storia della Letteratura Italiana*, todas las palabras, "vengan de donde vengan y sean las que sean: toscanas, locales y forasteras, nobles y plebeyas, poéticas y prosaicas, ásperas y dulces, sencillas o sonoras (Mario Baratto, 301, nota 11). Por su lado, Mario Baratto observa que no se trata sólo de un hablado, si no de un juego sobre el hablado (Mario Baratto, 301).

El anti-academismo y la crítica sardónica del lenguaje escrito anquilosado y dogmático son evidentes en los dos textos. Frente a una forma de escritura esclerosada y tradicional, el lenguaje de nuestros dos autores sugiere una alternativa, más a tono con la realidad romana de aquellos años tan agitados. Podemos, quizá, en nuestras próximas líneas examinar la función de esta escritura híbrida que permaneció en equilibrio entre la estructura novelista y la representación teatral.

La ciudad de Roma asume en el seno de la narrativa delicadiana, la función de una plataforma teatral, vasta caja de resonancia en la cual se entretejen las réplicas de los personajes, bajo la batuta del "auctor". Por otro lado, este mismo "auctor" distorsiona muy levemente la realidad, de manera que el lector apenas lo percibe: recurso muy hábil para poder encerrar en la selección de los topónimos romanos, la parte de cazurrismo que el "discreto lector" advierte a medida que va conociendo mejor a la heroína delicadiana y a su inigualable compañero de aventuras. La pareja invita al lector a seguirla, paso a paso, a través de una Roma "dominguera" y placentera, mediante un itinerario previamente trazado por el ingenioso "auctor". De esta manera tenemos dentro del texto un "collage" de los distintos lugares y puntos de interés "turístico" para dar al lector una visión parcializada de la Ciudad Eterna, haciendo hincapié en aquellos lugares donde imperan la prostitución, la sífilis y las transacciones nebulosas y deshonestas. El "auctor" está delimitando, en definitiva, el radio de acción de la bella andaluza. El itinerario de Lozana por las calles romanas se asimila estrechamente a la escritura del autor, escritura que "echa una mirada" por todos los rincones, filtra el mínimo ruido, recalca las muecas y los vicios de una ciudad que el lector-oyente romano capta en seguida.

Frente a este fondo de la ciudad visto por Lozana, tenemos el escenario romano de Nanna, espacio más complejo antes que nada porque Aretino introduce la representación teatral en el seno de la narración. Nanna actúa, recuerda y narra a la vez. Así llega a ser una narradora-espectadora-figurante-actriz. El lector-oyente de *I ragionamenti* se encuentra proyectado al centro de un ingenioso escenario circular ideado por el autor toscano. Oigamos la reacción de Nanna al momento de entrar en una sala del convento:

"Nanna.—Noi andammo in una camera terrena ampia e fresca e tutta dipinta.
Antonia.—Che dipinture c'erano? La penitenza della quaresima o che?
Nanna.—Che penitenza: le dipinture erano tali che avrieno intertemito a mirarle gli ipocriti. La camera avea quattro facce: nella prima era la vita di Santa Nafissa. . . Nella seconda c'è la istoria Masetto di Lampolecchio. Nella terza ci erano (se ben mi ricordo) tutte le suore che fur mai di quello ordine, con i loro amanti appresso e i figlioli nati di esse. . . Nell'ultimo quadro ci erano dipinti tutti i modi e tutte le vie che si può

chiavare e farsi chiavare; e sono obbligate le moniche prima che le si mettino in campo con gli amici loro di provare di stare negli atti vivi che stanno le dipinte. . ." (Pietro Aretino, I-1, 14-16).

Este nuevo tipo de estructura teatral que presenta cuatro escenarios, es una idea muy ingeniosa de Aretino. Este concepto teatral que consiste en inmiscuir al público con la obra misma, en una especie de espectáculo total convierte al espectador en un personaje que mira y que es mirado, a la misma vez, por otros personajes en una sucesión de miradas que crean el principio del laberinto de los juegos de espejos. Esta dimensión especular de la ficción es un recurso teatral que desarrollarán dramaturgos del siglo XX como Brecht, Pirandello e Ionesco. Aretino retoma la misma idea algunas páginas después, cuando Nanna se pone a espiar las "justas" amorosas entre el padre general de la orden, el canónigo, la madre superior, tres monjes y cuatro monjas. Nos encontramos de nuevo en una celda ubicada en el centro de otras cuatro. Las paredes de la celda central están agrietadas intencionalmente, de forma que uno puede ver y a la misma vez ser observado. Esta inter-visión se repite en todas las demás celdas. Nanna nos explica claramente como funciona este sistema de "voyeurisme" recíproco:

"Nanna. . . Egli (il baccelliere) mi condusse in una cameretta posta nel mezzo di tutte le camere: le quali erano divise da un ordine di semplici mattoni; e cosí male male incalcinate le commessure del muro che ogni poco d'occhio che si dava ai fessi, si potea vedere ciò che si operava dentro gli alberghetti di ciascuna" (Idem. I-1, I7).

Sin embargo, algunos días después, Nanna se entera de que, si ella estaba mirando a lo demás, otras personas la miraban durante sus relaciones sexuales:

"Nanna.—Non potea contener i ghigni vedendo quelle che erano la notte prima gite in carnafau: e domesticata in pochi dì con tutte, fui chiarita che sì come i' visi altri, altri vide me: cioè in tresca con il baccelliere." (Idem. I-1, 41).

El escritor toscano intuyó en seguida el potencial de teatralidad que llevaba la Nanna. Las técnicas de histriona que implanta aquella mujer en sus historias echan un puente entre el teatro y la narración. No olvidemos que esta transposición que Aretino dejó inacabada, la desarrollará Pirandello cuatro siglos más tarde, realizando una versión teatral para la mayoría de sus *Novelle per un anno.*[2]

Como lo descubrieron Lozana y Rampín en medio del discurso literario de la obra que integran, Nanna advierte a su hija Pippa, que no son nada más que puros constructos verbales, meros personajes de ficción. Sin embargo, ellos no padecen la náusea existencial que sufren los personajes cervantinos. Por consiguiente, Nanna y Lozana van tomando conciencia de que no tienen ni cuerpo ni religión, ni patria ni familia, ni sentido moral. Lo único que las salva es el virtuosismo de actrices histriónicas, listas a imitar, engañar, mimar, actuar, recitar, hasta crear personajes dentro de la narración. En efecto, ¿quién es Jaqueta en el mamotreto LV de *La Lozana*? Una creación de la misma heroína, que la inventa y la dramatiza frente al lector:

"Lozana.—Amor mio, Coridón dulce, recipe el remedio: va, compra una veste de villana que sea blanca y unas mangas verdes, y vayte descalzo y suzio loqueando, que todos te llamarán loca, y di que te llamen Jaqueta, que vas por el mundo reprehendiendo las cosas mal hechas. Y si te vieres solo con essa tu amante Polidora, haz vista que siempre lloras y si te demandare por qué, dile: "Porque jamás mi nación fue villana. Sabe que soy gentildona breciana, y me vi que podía estar par a par con Diana, y con cualquier otra dama que en el mundo fuesse estada." Ella te replicará que tú le digas: "¿Por qué vas ansí, mi cara Jaqueta?" Tú le dirás: "Cara madona, voy por el mundo reprochando las cosas mal hechas. Sabed que mi padre me casó con un viejo como vuestro marido, calvo, floxo como un niño, y no me dió a un joven que me demandava siendo donzella, el cual se fue desperado, que voy por el mundo a buscarlo." Si ella te quiere bien, luego lo verás en su hablar, y si te cuenta a ti lo mismo, dile cómo otro día te partes a buscarlo." (LADA, LV, pp. 369-370).

¿Qué hace Nanna en cada momento de la narración? Se re-crea veinte años después o re-crea personajes, asumiendo por cada interpretación una máscara distinta, identificándose al máximo a su autor para criticar a los intelectuales que optaban por un lenguaje demasiado sofisticado y pedante, lo que ya había dejado de existir en su forma oral. En otras palabras, Aretino

---

[2] En Italia, hay que esperar a Luigi Pirandello para ver un autor transformar sus cuentos en representaciones teatrales. Consúltese el estudio de Gilbert Besetti, *Pirandello*, "Des nouvelles au théâtre."

rechaza una forma de hablar arcaica que no se oye por las calles de Roma. Sin embargo, la elaboración estilística es muy patente tanto en el texto del Flagelo de Príncipes como en el del escritor andaluz. Este afirma claramente en su "Dedicatoria" que la persona a quien el dedica su Lozana "toma plazer quando oye hablar en cossas de amor que deleytan a todo hombre" (LADA, "Dedicatoria," p. 69).

El retrato de la Lozana andaluza va a "deleitar a todo hombre," porque Lozana (y luego Nanna) no habla como una mujer, sino como les gustaría a los hombres que hablase la mujer. Nuestras dos protagonistas son puros objetos sexuales, fuentes generadoras de placer en las manos de sus autores-proxenetas-alcahuetes. Las dos mujeres encajan bien en la estructura de la Urbe, en la medida en que los autores asimilan al centro de la cristiandad a un vasto prostíbulo y que Lozana con su nariz roma es la imagen viva de la crisis que vive la ciudad papal y su sociedad algunos años antes y después del saco de 1527. La identificación de dichas mercenarias del amor con la ciudad se nota, además, en el paralelismo que existe entre sus aventuras y la adecuación de las dichas aventuras con los lugares donde se desarrollan. "Roma, città aperta," es un lugar-escenario limitado en su espacio, pero ilimitado en sus efectos acústicos.

Tanto Delicado como Aretino juegan con la delimitación del área considerada: la ciudad y sus infinitas combinaciones auditivas: sonidos, ruidos, risas, canciones y conversaciones de las personas que deambulan por las calles. Y puesto que las que pasan más tiempo en las calles y a la intemperie son las prostitutas, nos proponemos ahora contrastar la visión de la ciudad en ambos escritores, a través de las amigas de infortunio que gravitan alrededor de Lozana y Nanna. Si Aretino deleita al lector-oidor con largas descripciones pictóricas, Delicado, en cambio, nos hace ver cosas a través de los personajes. Sin embargo, estos personajes resultan maquetas incompletas y parciales como en La Celestina o Liber Pamphilus. Se privilegia el oído dentro de la tradición literaria europea y española aún oral.[3] Aretino en cambio,

---

[3] No hay duda de que Francisco Delicado privilegia el oído puesto que durante la Edad media y gran parte del Renacimiento el receptor del mensaje escrito era oidor y la lectura se hacía en voz alta. Como bien lo comenta el autor en la primera oración de su "Dedicatoria," cuando se dirige al "Ilustre señor," todo lo que encontramos en La Lozana andaluza es digno de ser oído:
"Sabiendo yo que vuestra señoría toma el plazer quando oye hablar en cossas de amor, que deleytan a todo ombre y máxime quando siente dezir de personas que mejor se, supieron dar la manera para administrar las cosas a el pertenecientes" (LADA, 69).
A propósito de ésta relación que se establece entre oralidad literaria, ciudad y

permite a Nanna explayarse en la descripción visual y acústica de la ciudad y su gente, ya que pertenece a una tradición literaria que se inscribe en la línea de pensamiento que proviene de Bocacio, Masuccio Salernitano, Straparola, entre otros.

Si Lozana se dedica a la prostitución no es sólo por el acto venal en sí, esta mujer está dominada por el deseo de gozar sexualmente, y es obvio que detrás de la comercialización de su cuerpo, permanece la hembra que tiene ganas de vivir plenamente su vida. Es una mujer en todo el sentido de la palabra y por tal razón, cuando un amante no está a su altura, no vacila en delatarlo. Escuchemos la conversación entre el viejo Germán y Lozana en el mamotreto XXVI:

"Germán.—Va qu'eres necio, sácale la conserva de melón que enviaron ayer las monjas lombardas, y tráele de mi vino.

Lozana.—Por el alma de mi padre que ya sé que sois alixandro, que si fuésede español, no seriades proveído de melón, sino de buenas razones. Señor, con vos estaría toda mi vida, salvo que ya sabéis que aquella señora quiere barbiponientes y no jubileos.

---

estructuras sociales, pensamos que sería oportuno suministrar algunas consideraciones de Margit Frenk:

"Todo se sabe por el oído, por un oído que ve; "para el gusto basta oýr' comenta Urgada" (114).

Algunas páginas después, escribe que en la primera mitad del siglo la poesía, el teatro y la novela parecen haber tenido un público predominantemente aristocrático. A partir de mediados de siglo su radio de acción se ensancha. Es justamente el momento en que la incipiente burguesía comercial castellana experimenta "un ascenso . . . prometedor', como dice Dominguez Ortiz. . . (117).

También Robert Mandrou no falta a señalar esta característica de la primacía del oído en la receptividad de los textos. "El crítico francés observa lo siguiente:

"En cela, l'époque moderne prolonge un caractére essentiel de la civilisation médiévale; non sans un brin de paradoxe, puisque l'imprimé en incessante progression exprime apparemment la faveur croissante de la lecture: mais dans tous les milieux sociaux, elle se fait encore à haute et intelligible voix; elle est à fois lecture et audition. L'information reste principalement auditive: même les grands de ce monde écoutent plus qu'ils ne lisent; ils sont entourés de conseillers qui leur parlent, qui leur fournissent leur savoir par l'oreille, qui lisent devant eux. Dans les assemblées d'administrateurs, les conseillers des rois et des princes portent tout naturellement et fréquemment le titre d'auditeurs; et à veillée, dans les humbles chaumières paysannes, c'est encore le récit qui nourrit les pensée et les imaginations. Enfin, même ceux qui lisent volontiers, les humanistes, sont accoutumés de le faire aussi en compagnie — et entendent leur texte. "A cette primauté il y a tout d'abord une raison d'ordre religieux: c'est la Parole de Dieu qui est l'autorité suprême de l'Eglise. La Foi elle-même est audition': (76-77).

Germán.—¿Qué me decís señora Lozana? Que más caricias me hace que se yo fuese su padre.

Lozana.—Pues mire vuestra merced que ella me dijo que quería bien a vuestra merced porque parecía a su agüelo, y no le quitaba tajuda." (LADA, XXVI, p. 223).

Nanna, en cambio, es una auténtica "máquina" que sirve para ofrecer placer. Ella, como su padre espiritual, es demasiado calculadora y cínica para poder enamorarse. Si Lozana declara que se enamoró de Diomedes, y en cierto sentido le guarda amor y fidelidad a Rampín, Nanna es una mujer que encontró su camino sola y que eliminó al esposo. La bella romana está más allá del escándalo. Como su creador, esta protagonista se ha hecho un nombre a base de ello, su fama se nutre de los golpes bajos, del chantaje, de la depravación del odio, de los rencores y de algunas amistades claves. Es una mujer que vive con coherencia una determinada situación social.

Roma está literalmente plagada por una gran cantidad de prostitutas, al punto que se ha convertido en la capital del juego y del sexo. El lector encuentra que existe en la ciudad una jerarquía de la prostitución muy bien estructurada, la cual se extiende desde la ramera de la calle hasta las cortesanas de mucho vuelo. Tal jerarquía está tan ligada con los intereses económicos del Vaticano que la ciudad romana llega a tomar la apariencia de un vasto lupanar. La ciudad depravada se convierte así, en un suburbio de Madrid,[4] puesto que la capital del cristianismo había caído en las manos del clero español. Es casi natural entonces, ver al vicario andaluz asumir tanta familiaridad con su heroína. Los vemos coquetear, beber y tener relaciones libidinosas juntos.

Por otro lado, el repertorio de prostitutas suplido por el balijero y recitado con ritmo de letanía, nos hace pensar en los interminables parlamentos de Nanna, quien adapta el flujo narrativo y oratorio a la cadencia respiratoria. La Roma-teatro de Nanna es más cotidiana, más doméstica: los lugares que ella describe son los que ve todos los días. Ahora, la Roma que va descubriendo Lozana, es una ciudad más vinculada con su grandeza

---

[4] A propósito de esta característica, Francisco Márquez villanueva opina que "a pesar de su fondo romano, La Lozana no ocurre fuera de un tablado español" (87).
Por otro lado, en el mamotréto XII Lozana hace referencia a la inmigración de los españoles a Roma; además establece un paralelo entre España y Roma:
"Lozana.—¡Por mi vida que es cosa de saber y ver, que dizen que en aquel tiempo no havía dos españoles en Roma y agora ay tantos! Verná tiempo que no avrá ninguno y dirán "Roma mísera', como dizen 'España mísera'." (LADA, 126).

pasada. Delicado es más sensible a una Roma histórica y clásica, la de los visitantes extranjeros. Hace alusión a los monumentos famosos, irreductibles fantasmas de una gloria ya inexistente. El escritor cordobés, agudo observador "turístico," queda impresionado por la riqueza cultural y las bellezas artísticas de lo que se va a convertir en el nuevo universo cotidiano con el que Lozana se va a identificar. Ya entendemos por qué nuestras dos protagonistas son inigualables en su personalidad y belleza, y es sólo porque son íntimamente asimiladas con Roma/amor, ciudad cuya belleza y vicios no tienen comparación. En otros términos, el retrato de Lozana y el retrato de Nanna son dos partes de un cuadro ejecutado "urbi et orbi," que es, en el fondo, el retrato de Roma. En éste, domina el mecanismo de la astucia, una psicología de la prostituta adquirida y aplicada durante "peregrinaciones" peripatéticas, la estrategia de la araña, la malicia del zorro, un dominio inconfundible del lenguaje, a tal punto que pensamos que, si estas dos meretrices poseen un don de la palabra tan alto, la visión de la ciudad que tenemos, sirve más para ajustar cuentas con sus detractores (especialmente en el caso de Aretino) que para reflejar objectivamente una realidad de todos los días. Sin embargo, a pesar de unas cuantas analogías, las dos heroínas presentan algunas marcadas diferencias. Notamos que Lozana ama su oficio y es más vital, siente placer y aun se enamora; Nanna es más maquiavélica, odia o desprecia a sus clientes, está curtida para el amor y aún para el placer.

"L'ineptie c'est de vouloir conclure," escribía Flaubert; no obstante, debemos llevar nuestro estudio hacia un punto final. Hemos tratado de delinear una visión romana captada por cada escritor a través de las mirads clínicas de Lozana y Nanna. Miradas que nos han llevado a aludir a la presencia de Roma como personaje desencarnado pero omnipresente en las dos obras. Esta ciudad se percibe como un espacio-escenario ideal para establecer un vínculo positivo entre narración novelesca y representación teatral. Detrás de estos dos retratos de la ciudad papal, surge el retrato personal de Delicado y de Aretino como individuos que llevan una vida poco edificante, en el seno de una sociedad que promueve este tipo de vida silenciosa. Ahora, lo que es interesante recalcar es que detrás de cada autor, surge el retrato del escritor frente a su trabajo escritural, no como artista, sino como artesano, como orfebre de la oración con los efectos inmediatos del lenguaje sobre el oído y la imaginación del lector-oidor.

Para terminar, debemos confesar que lo que hicieron Delicado y Aretino con su vida personal pertenece estrictamente a la historia del siglo

XVI, mientras que lo que escribieron en sus respectivas obras capta la atención de la crítica literaria de los albores del siglo XXI.

The Catholic University of America

BIBLIOGRAFIA

Aretino, Pietro. *Sei Giornate,* Commento a cura di Giovanni Aquilecchia, Bari: Laterza, 1969.

Baratto, Mario. *Teatro y luchas sociales: Ruzante Aretino, Goldoni,* Barcelona: Ediciones Peninsula, 1977.

Bosetti, Gilbert. *Pirandello,* Paris: Bordas, 1971.

Delicado, Francisco. *El retrato de la Lozana andaluza,* Edición de Bruno Damiani y Giovanni Allegra, Madrid: José Porrúa Turanzas, S.A., 1975.

Frenk, Margit. "Lectores y oidores", Conferencia Plenaria VIImo Congreso Internacional de Hispanistas, Venecia, Italia: 1980. "La difusión oral de la literatura en el Siglo de Oro".

Gilman, Stephen. *Celestina, arte y escritura* Madrid: Taurus, 1977.

Mandrou, Robert. *Introduction a la France moderne 1500-1640.* Paris: Editions Albin Michel, 1974.

Márquez-Villanueva, Francisco. "El mundo converso de la Lozana andaluza", *Archivo Hispalense,* Sevilla: Archivo Histórico, Literario, Artístico, 1973.

Influence italiane sulla genesi e struttura del romanzo picaresco spagnolo

Giulio Massano

La letteratura picaresca é un genere letterario internazionale. Nonostante che le opere picaresche abbiano raggiunto il loro massimo splendore, sia nella creazione di un carattere letterario proprio, come nella descrizione di questo carattere in relazione alla società, nei secoli XVI e XVII in Spagna, le loro origini non si possono stabilire con precisione come appartenenti alla Spagna o ad altri paesi europei. Appare pure difficoltoso precisare il período storico in cui la figura letteraria del pícaro si definisce come tale nella novela, poesía e teatro.[1] La crítica tradizionale ha trattato di vedere nel carattere picaresco tracce di personaggi burleschi della letteratura classica, specialmente dell, *Asino d'oro* di Apuleio, del *Satyricon* di Petronio e del teatro di Arístofane.

Questi tentativi si giustificano solo nel fatto che stabiliscono una continuità di figure letterarie nella letteratura occidentale, ma non possono spiegare la fisionomia unica del romanzo picaresco spagnolo del 1500 e

---

[1] Non è mia intenzione analizzare qui le opinioni dei vari critici sul concetto di picaresca, perchè gli studi specializzati sull'argomento sono abbondantissimi. Mi limito a citare un'opera che compendia le numerose posizioni critiche sul soggetto e che discute, in modo chiaro ed accessibile, le caratteristiche che furono considerate parte integrante dalla critica tradizionale, cioè: la narrazione autobiografica, la descrizione pessimistica ed unilaterale della società, la degradazione morale e psicológica del protagonista, il problema della sopravvivenza, dell'onore e della rispettabilità. Vedere Joseph Ricapito, *Toward a Definiation of the Picaresque...* (Ann Arbor: University Microfilms, 1964).

82

1600. Gli scrittori spagnoli raggiunsero nel genere letterario che trattiamo, una perfezione difficile da uguagliare ed ogni altra influenza esterna li aiutò solamente a concepire il personaggio del pícaro ed a strutturare il romanzo picaresco nella forma particolare che conosciamo.

Si giustifica allora, date queste concessioni, lo studio presente? Senza dubbio, se si considerano i presupposti seguenti, cioè: 1— la originalità spagnola nel presentare un personaggio che incarna tutto il settore di una societa marginata e senza onore, 2— il debito degli scrittori picareschi verso la letteratura burlesca italiana che contiene numerose caratterizzazioni e caratteristiche che il pícaro spagnolo farà poi sue, 3— l'inserimento nel romanzo picaresco spagnolo di avventure già conosciute ed apparse nel grande "corpus" della novela italiana, e 4— la imitazione degli autori spagnoli della tecnica italiana di intromettere nella descrizione dello svolgimento d'un episodio, alcune avventure piacevoli che non sono affatto legate al suo sviluppo totale, con lo scopo unico di divertire il lettore. Questi ultimi tre punti, che costituiscono aspetti non indifferenti del romanzo picaresco spagnolo, offrono, a mio parere, sufficenti ragioni per stabilire e precisare le influenze italiane sia sul concetto di pícaro stesso, come sulla tecnica strutturale del romanzo spagnolo.

Le letteratura italiana del Medioevo e del Rinascimento fu ben conosciuta ed ammirata in tutta Europa. Quasi tutti gli scrittori italiani, da Dante al meno importante, furono tradotti o ristampati nella lingua originale verso la fine del 1500.[2] Le influenze maggiori della letteratura italiana si notano, però, in Spagna, dove anni di strette relazioni politiche, economiche, sociali e diplomatiche, facilitarono lo scambio culturale. I maggiori scrittori spagnoli, tra cui Cervantes, Francisco de Quevedo, Vicente Espinel e Mateo Alemán, viaggiarono per l'Italia, ne assorbirono gli influssi rinascentisti e fecero allo

---

[2]   Accenniamo ad alcuni esempi della popolarità della letteratura italiana in Europa. In Francia il *Decameron* fu tradotto nel 1503 e le *Novelle* di Matteo Bandello nel 1573. Opere minori come gli *Hecatommithi* di Giraldi Cinthio e il *Pentamerone* di Giovanni Basile apparirono pure in questo periodo; il primo nel 1583 e il secondo nel 1600 Anche in Inghilterra gli scrittori italiani del genere novelesco raggiunsero una popolarità immensa: "I nostri narratori furono i tesori nascosti nei "closets' dei lettori e delle lettrici mondane, nonostante le deplorazioni dei puritani che vedevano contaminare, come diceva St. Gosson, 'the old manners' della vecchia Inghilterra 'with foreign delight.'" Cit. da Antero Meozzi, p. 190. La fama dei novellisti italiani era stata promossa dalla pubblicazione del *Palace of Pleasure* di William Painter (1567) che presentava, tradotte all'inglese, 16 novelle di Boccaccio, 25 di Bandello, 2 di Giraldi Cinthio e I di Giovan Francesco Straparola. Titolo originale dell'opera: William Painter (1540-1594), *The Palace of Pleasure: Elizabethan Versions of Italian and French Novels from Boccaccio. Bandello. Cinthio. Straparola, etc.*

stesso tempo conoscere nelle corti italiane il loro talento.[3] In questo scambio reciproco la Spagna si arrìchì di umanisti di sommo valore come Lucio Marineo Sículo e di numerosi italiani specializzati nell'arte della stampa, nella lavorazione dell'oro e nel commercio della lana.

Dalla fine del 1400 le traduzioni spagnole di collezioni di novelle italiane si susseguono a ritmo notevole, specialmente se si considerano i metodi primitivi della stampa dell'epoca. Un semplice elenco di opere di scrittori italiani di maggiore e minore importanza del tempo, dimostrerà questo fenomeno unico nelle relazioni culturali tra nazioni. Il *Decameron* fu tradotto per la prima volta anonimamente nel 1492; traduzioni posterior apparirono a Seviglia nel 1496, a Toledo nel 1524 e a Valladolid nel 1550. Vicente Mills Godínez, discendente da una famiglia di stampatori genovesi che aveva già in precedenza pubblicato le opere di Boccaccio a Medina del Campo, s'incaricò nel 1589 della traduzione di alcune *Novelle* di Matteo Bandello. Appaiono pure, in questo periodo (1583) traduzioni delle *Piacevoli notti* di Giovan Francesco Straparola e dei *Dialoghi* di Pietro Aretino negli anni 1547, 1548 e 1607.

Raggiunge pure nel secolo XVI in Spagna un elevato grado di popolarità la poesia comica e burlesca di Luigi Pulci e di Teofilo Folengo. Il *Morgante Maggiore* di Pulci fu tradotto da un anonimo nel 1533 ed il *Marguttino*, continuazione del *Morgante* fu reso accessibile agli Spagnoli dal poeta di Valencia Jerónimo de Adner nel 1533. Una traduzione spagnola della *Trebisonda Historiata* (1526) dell'italiano Francesco Tromba, contiene, oltre ai "grandes hechos de Roldán, don Reynaldos, etc." il *Baldus* di Folengo e una quantità ragguardevole di poemi epici e cavallereschi.[4]

Anche se il numero delle traduzioni di per se sarebbe sufficiente per significare la grande popolarità della letteratura italiana in Spagna, le traduzioni stesse non danno il quadro completo per il fatto che i lettori spagnoli conoscevano sufficientemente l'italiano per leggerne le opere nell'originale. Conferma Marcelino Menéndez y Pelayo: "Del número de

---

[3]   La bibliografía degli studi comparativi tra Spagna e Italia è assai voluminosa e le opere più importanti consultate per questo studio appaiono nell'elenco delle opere citate.

[4]   Queste informazioni storiche possono essere ampliate consultando la bibliografia specializzata di José Simon Díaz, *Bibliografía de la literatura hispánica* (Madrid: Consejo superior de investigaciones científicas, 1953), III e IV. Opera di carattere generale che presenta una quantitá eccezionale di dati storici è pure quella di Marcelino Menéndez y Pelayo, *Orígenes de la novela* (Santander: Aldus, 1943), XIII, 223, 226; vol. XV, 4; *Antología de poetas ricos castellanos* (Santander: Aldus, 1944), XVII, 394 e seg.

estas versiones. . . no puede juzgarse . . . el grado de la influencia italiana. Era tan familiar (l'italiano) a los españoles que la mayor parte de los aficionados a la lectura amena gozaba de estos libros en su lengua original, desdeñando, con razón, las traducciones que solían ser tan incorrectas y adocenadas."

Non appare affatto sorprendente che gran parte della letteratura italiana fosse cosi popolare ed accessibile ai lettori spagnoli, se si considera che i generi letterari più diffusi erano generalmente diretti a divertire più che ad elevare lettori attraverso opere dai fini didascalici o estetici. Le *Novelle* con il loro soggetti arrischiati e la poesía burlesca intaccavano due dei mondi più rispettati e solidi del tempo; nelle *Novelle* si satirizzava la vita matrimoniale e si presentavano alternative alla rigidità dell'unione monogamica, e nella poesia burlesca si faceva luce su un mondo cavalleresco fin troppo diffuso ed arrogante e se ne presentavano gli aspetti più comici e sgradevoli.

Questa indubbia presenza italiana nelle lettere spagnole, lasciò tracce sia nella concezione di caratteri con attitudini nuove verso la società, come sarà poi il pícaro, sia come nel dimostrare una nuova tecnica narrativa che si concentrava in brevi, ma completi episodi della vita, come apparirà nei numerosi episodi intercalati dei romanzi picareschi. A continuazione si determinerà allora: 1— quali aspetti della letteratura italiana facilitarono la creazione del pícaro spagnolo, e 2— quali novelle italiane entrarono con pochi o adirittura con nessun cambio, nella grande collezione del romanzo picaresco spagnolo.

1— Figure con tracce picaresche nella letteratura italiana del 1400 e l500

Si trovano nella letteratura italiana opere che possono aver condotto gli scrittori spagnoli a concepire la figura del pícaro. Le creazioni letterarie principal sono, senza dubbio, il *Morgante* (1478) di Luigi Pulci e il *Baldus* (1517) di Teofilo Folengo. In ambi poemi abbondano passaggi realistici e burleschi ed i protagonisti Morgante, Rinaldo, ecc. passano attraverso un numero eccezionale di sofferenze, umiliazioni, come sopporteranno più tardi i pícaros spagnoli. In molte circostanze il cavaliere Orlando è oggetto di derisione e dileggio da parte di giovani adolescenti che vedono in lui il rappresentante d'una umanità povera e senza dignità. In un mondo che non vuole capire il suo comportamento, Orlando perde involontariamente il desiderio di lottare per la sua amata e così riguadagnare il suo stato sociale. Si constata inoltre un altro aspetto picaresco nel *Morgante*; la determinazione di uno dei protagonisti, nel nostro caso, Rinaldo, di condurre una vita da malandrino al margine della legge "Io vo' che tutto il paese rubiamo e che di mascalzon vita tegnamo" (XI, 19).

L'episodio più convincente per il nostro scopo, s'incontra pero nell'avventura di Margutte. Pulci lascia ad un lato, la descrizione di battaglie, di dame, di reami fantastici, per presentarci l'incontro dell'eroe Morgante con un forestiero di nome Margutte. L'inserzione della figura di Margutte nel mondo cavalleresco di Pulci non è arbitraria e senza ragione; corrisponde invece all'intenzione di creare un anti-eroe ed un'immagine negativa in un mondo rigurgitante di eroi, cavalieri e dame. Vediamo il rompersi di una tradizione cavalleresca ben radicata con la presentazione, fatta con un tono approvante, di un fuorilegge conscio della sua forza distruttiva nella società.

Margutte attraverso la narrazione della sua vita a Morgante, accentua la sua nascita illegittima (XVIII, 112), spiega la sua intenzione di condurre una vita spensierata e senza lavoro (XVIII, 119) e di sopravvivere per mezzo del ladrocinio, estorsione e violenza (XVIII, 119, 133, 134). L'ideale di Margutte è negativo, egoista in chiara opposizione alla maggioranza dei personaggi che popolano il poema di Pulci. Margutte è così orgoglioso della sua vita bassa e miserevole che non la combierebbe con nessun altra più nobile ed agiata anche se ne avesse l'opportunità (XVIII, 115, 132). La stessa attitudine verso la vita apparirà con frequenza enorme nei romanzi picareschi spagnoli.[5]

Luigi Pulci non arriva fino al punto di dimostrare che la vita di Margutte è il risultato diretto della sua nascita illegittima, della sua mancanza d'educazione e della sua marginazione sociale; in più, l'episodio intiero e avvolto in un'atmosfera leggera, burlesca ed umoristica. Margutte non è certo il prototipo completo del pícaro spagnolo e la descrizione del suo modo di morire come conseguenza del troppo ridere al vedere una scimmia che si mette e toglie i suoi stivali, sarebbe sufficiente per convincerci del contrario (XIX, 147). Pur tuttavia, alcune caratteristiche che sono condizioni quasi universali del romanzo picaresco, come la narrazione autobiografica, l'importanza data alla

---

[5] Cito solo due esempi riportati dallo studioso Alfonso Bonilla y San Martín. Il poeta del 1600 Pedro Laínez si riferisce in termini orgogliosi e spregiudicati alla vita picaresca: "Gozar de libertad, vivir contento,/ soñarse rey vistiéndose de andrajos,/ comer faisanes siendo solo ajos..." La stessa attitudine si constata nel poema La vida del pícaro dello stesso periodo, d'autore sconosciuto: "Muy largo procedía y corto quedo/ en alabar la vida que codicio,/ enemiga de faustos y miedo/ ...sólo el pícaro muere bien logrado,/ que, desde que nació, nada desea,/ y ansí lo tiene todo acaudalado." "La vida del pícaro," Révue Hispanique. IX (1902), 295-330.

nascita illegittima, il desiderio di vivere senza leggi, e la continua atmosfera di delinquenza, appaiono già chiaramente nel *Morgante*.

Un'altra fonte italiana che può aver facilitato la genesi della figura del pícaro negli scrittori spagnoli, si trova nel *Baldus* di Teofilo Folengo. In questo poema burlesco, scritto in latino maccheronico, Baldus, l'eroe principale, ingaggia servizi di tre palafrenieri, i cui nomi: Fracassus, Cingar e Falchetto, già indicano le loro origini, educazione e intenzioni (IV, vv. 53-146). Teofilo Folengo non definisce però sufficientemente questi personaggi e quindi non raggiungono un personalità picaresca matura. Servono principalmente a creare l'atmosfera di un mondo paradossale e illogico in cui l'inganno, la mancanza d'etica e la bugia sono le uniche vie della sopravvivenza. I tre palafrenieri vedono il mondo in una prospettiva rovesciata, in cui i valori reali non sono quelli cavallereschi, ma quelli illegali dei delinquenti.

Come già detto, le opere di Pulci e Folengo non creano la figura completa del pícaro. L'intenzione degli autori italiani era di burlarsi dell'epica, del suo mondo monolitico e inaccessibile e della sua struttura sociale, e, per di più, d'introdurre nella letteratura troppo intenta al panegirico, gli aspetti realli di una delinquenza già diffusissima. La stessa intenzione, con ovvie variazioni dovute alla personalità degli scrittori, ai cambi di percezione artistica e ad una differente società apparirà negli autori picareschi spagnoli e il loro pícaro sarà veicolo adatto per tale presentazione.

2—Le novelle italiane intercalate nel romanzo picaresco spagnolo

Le numerose novelle italiane, incorporate con differenti gradi d'importanza ed unità nel grande fiume del romanzo picaresco spagnolo, sono, senza dubbio, le fonti più convincenti dell'influenza italiana.[6] Queste novelle e favole sono introdotte nelle composizioni spagnole in due modi: 1 — come parte intrinseca della narrazione; cioè, nella sua attuazione diaria, il pícaro è protagonista in avventure già descritte ed ampliamente elaborate anni precedenti dai novellieri italiani, diventando con questa forma, le novele

---

[6] Non analizzeremo in questa sezione influenze di carattere generale e concettuale che possono esistere tra la letteratura italiana e il romanzo picaresco spagnolo. Studi al riguardo già sono stati fatti. Riferisco solo uno di Joseph Fucilla che stabilisce la relazione di un poema di Berni ("Capitolo a Messer Hieronimo Fracastoro") con un passaggio de *La vida del Buscón* (libro I, cap. XIII) di Francisco Quevedo. Vedere Joseph Fucilla, *op. cit.*, PP. 135-136.

italiane, parte integrante della vita del carattere e 2 — come parte estrinseca della narrazione; cioè, nel suo racconto autobiografico, il protagonista lascia ad un lato, per un breve periodo lo svolgimento della sua vita, per introdurre, con lo scopo esclusivo di divertire ed alleviare lo spirito, alcuni episodi piacevoli che non hanno nesso alcuno con il protagonista stesso o suoi interlocutori. Molti degli episodi intercalati alla narrazione principale si possono incontrare nei novellieri italiani.

Al primo gruppo appartengono un racconto del *Lazarillo de Tormes*, quattro episodi del *Marcos de Obregón* e due avventure de *La desordenada codicia de los bienes agenos*. Al secondo, un racconto del *Guzmán de Alfarache* e numerose digressioni nella produzione di Alonso de Castillo Solórzano.

Di tutti i racconti d'origine italiana che hanno influito sul romanzo picaresco spagnolo, quello che è stato oggetto di maggiore attenzione da parte degli studiosi moderni è senza dubbio l'episodio del Buldero del *Lazarillo de Tormes* (Tratado V). Si farà qui solamente sunto delle conclusioni di un articolo scritto da Joseph Ricapito[7] che si estende nel comparare l'episodio del romanzo spagnolo con la novella quarta del *Novellino* di Masuccio Salernitano. Lo studioso stabilisce che l'autore del *Lazarillo* non imitò tutti gli aspetti della novela di Masuccio, ma piuttosto "adopted the tale on its own artistic and idological premises and extended it." L'anonimo, conclude l'articolo, deve a Masuccio la concezione dei caratteri e la struttura basica dell'avventura, ma poi "reworked the Italianate premises with a basis in a particular Spanish social situation." L'intenzione del *Lazarillo* era di criticare la società credulona e di satirizzare il clero profittatore e Masuccio gli offerse il canovaccio adatto.

Il numero maggiore di novelle d'ispirazione italiana del romanzo picaresco spagnolo appare nel *Marcos de Obregón* di Vicente Espinel. Lo scrittore spagnolo che viaggiò per anni in Italia, mescola senza reticenze avventure personali con episodi tratti dai novellieri italiani e perciò gli elementi autobiografici dell'opera sono di natura ibrida e discutibili.[8]

L'episodio che ha numerosi precedenti nella Letteratura italiana è quello del Doctor Sagredo y Doña Mergelina (928-934). Contiene la narrazione tutti gli elementi necessari per essere un'unità completa in se stessa, ma la sua

---

7   Joseph Ricapito, "*Lazarillo de Tormes* (chap. V) and Masuccio's Fourth *Novela.*" *Romance Philology*, XXIII (1970), 305-311.

8   George Haley, *Vicente Espinel and Marcos de Obregón* (Providence: Brown University Press, 1959), p. 94-95. Haley é uno dei migliori studiosi di Vicente Espinel e nell'analisi di questa sezione si utilizzeranno alcune conclusioni sue.

esistenza nel racconto dipende dalla connessione che ha con Marcos de Obregón. Varie novelle di Boccaccio possono offrire a Espinel la base per questa avventura (novela 10, giornata V; novela 2, giornata VII, novella 6, giornata VII). Esistono infatti importanti somiglianze tra i due racconti; enumeriamoli: 1 — Alcune mogli, deluse del comportamento poco amoroso de i loro mariti, invitano, mentre essi sono assenti, dei giovani amanti nelle loro stanze. 2 — i mariti tornano a casa senza preavviso e le mogli sono costrette a nascondere i loro amanti. 3 — Un animale (in Espinel un cane, in Boccaccio, un asino) con un comportamento inusitato fanno scoprire a mariti l'imbarazzante presenza degli amanti. 4 — Le mogli riescono a convincere i mariti che gli amanti sono innocenti. 5 — Mogli, mariti, amanti finiscono intorno ad una tavola cenando allegramente.

Lo scrittore spagnolo avrebbe potuto trarre l'episodio del Doctor Sagredo y Doña Mergelina da molti altri novellieri italiani; tra gli altri, da Giovanni Sercambi (novela 138), Ser Giovanni Fiorentino (novela 12), Matteo Bandello (novela 11), Pietro Aretino (*I Ragionamenti*) e Masuccio Salernitano (novela 3). Esistono variazioni tra gli scrittori italiani e Vicente Espinel nello sviluppo della trama dell'episodio, specialmente negli accorgimenti usati dalle mogli per giustificare a mariti la presenza nelle loro stanze dei giovani amanti, ma la similitudine più frequente e sconcertante sta nel finale di un episodio che avrebbe potuto conchiudersi tragicamente, cioè: tutti i protagonisti si rallegrano attorno ad una tavola imbandita e così dimenticano gelosie e bugie.

Vicente Espinel prende ispirazione di nuovo dal grande "corpus" delle novelle italiane negli episodi del cimitero e del pozzo (942, 1006). L'avventura del cimitero ha uno sviluppo comico relativamente comune alla novela italiana. Marcos, il protagonista è inviato da una signora, il giorno precedente alla quaresima, a comprare carne. Il giovane si dilunga e tornando à casa e scoperto dalla ronda. Impaurito perchè già la città era in silenzio preparandosi per mercoledì delle ceneri, Marcos nasconde i suoi acquisti in una tomba vicina, sperando di riprenderli appena passate le guardie. Quando torna alla tomba, la carne è sparita, ed in più, rumori spaventosi escono dal sepolcro scoperchiato. Terrorizzato dal pensiero che l'anima del morto o il diavolo stesso siano interessati nella carne, Marcos fugge, però più in avanti, riprende il colraggio pensando che se è il diavolo, alla vista della croce fuggirà. Il giovane torna alla tomba, arringa il demonio, sfodera la spada ed un gigantesco cane nero esce ululando dalla parte opposta. Lo scrittore Franco Sacchetti (novela 120) ha pure una quasi identica avventura nei suoi scritti, come pure, almeno nel concetto, Giovanni Boccaccio (novela 5, giornata II, novela 1, giornata IX, novela 10, giornata IV).

La famosa novella d'Andreuccio da Perugia è anche la base fondamentale per l'episodio del pozzo del *Marcos de Obregón*. Gli sviluppi e gli stratagemmi per liberarsi dal pozzo, usati dai protagonisti dei due episodi sono diversi, però l'idea, la localizzazione ed il risultato dell'avventura sono identici.

L'epica italiana, nel nostro caso, *L'Orlando Furioso* (926-944) offre a Vicente Espinel materiale per l'avventura d'Aurelio e la moglie (1044-1047). In questo successo, più che negli altri già visti, perfino i dettagli minori sono copiati direttamente dal poeta italiano. Nel racconto gli scrittori mettono in rilievo le disastrose conseguenze dell'eccessiva gelosia dei mariti che scoprendo un estraneo nella propria casa, uccidono o puniscono crudelmente le loro mogli, senza cerziorarsi in precedenza della loro innocenza o colpevolezza. In più, in ambe le opere, i protagonisti, nell'*Orlando*, Rinaldo, ed in *Marcos de Obregón*, Marcos stesso, traggono la morale e giudicano severamente le condotta dei mariti, accecati da una inguista passione. Un tema identico con tragiche conclusioni si può trovare nel *Decameron* (336-339) ed un altro, con conclusioni più umane, negli *Hecatommithi* (43-48).

Dall'analisi dell'uso dei racconti italiani di Vicente Espinel, si possono trarre due conclusioni: 1 — Lo spagnolo, più che nessun altro scrittore picaresco conosceva i novellieri: italiani, e 2 — le avventure che lo spagnolo afferma di essergli successe personalmente, non lo sono affatto, ma già erano successe a personaggi vissuti nei secoli anteriori e già avevano dilettato in precedenza i lettori italiani.

Il romanzo dalle accentuate caratteristiche picaresche *La desordenada codicia de los bienes agenos* (1619) di Carlos García, uno spagnolo che viveva a Parigi, contiene un episodio che proviene, nella sua totalità, da due novellieri Gerolamo Morlini (29-31) e Giovan Francesco Straparola (202-204). Alla fine del capitolo VII Carlos García narra come un ladro riesce a rubare dei capponi e galline ad un contadino, senza dover ricorrere alla violenza, ma usando solo l'astuzia. Dopo aver mercanteggiato con il contadino il prezzo degli animali domestici, il ladro convince il contadino a seguirlo a un convento, perchè colà il padre confessore glieli pagherà, giacchè essi furono comprati per i frati. Il contadino di buona voglia segue il ladro alla chiesa del convento. Il ladro che ha già in possesso capponi e le galline, s'avvicina ad un confessionale e chiede al frate che confessi il contadino appena possibile, perchè, dice al sacerdote, il povero villano vive assai lontano dalla parrocchia, la Pasqua s'avvicina e per di più è da lungo tempo che non osserva il precetto della confessione pasquale. Il frate accondiscende e manifesta la sua intenzione muovendo capo in segno affermativo. Stabilita la confessione, il ladro scompare con i pennuti. Quando arriva il suo turno, il contadino si precipita al confessionale per ricevere la sua ricompensa dal sacerdote, e quest'ultimo che è all'oscuro della compra dei capponi e delle galline, invita il contadino ad inginocchiarsi ed a pentirsi. Il contadino rifiuta, il confessore pensa che sia un indemoniato ed abbia bisogno di un esorcismo, ed in mezzo alla confusione, urla ed intervento dei fedeli presenti, si scopre che il contadino è stato solennemente ingannato dal ladro. Mossi a pietà, i presenti pagano gli animali al povero burlato.

La ragione che spinse Carlos García ad incorporare l'avventura nel suo romanzo, fu forse l'opinione generale del tempo che riteneva che gli spagnoli fossero superiori agli altri popoli nell'arte del furto e della vita vagabonda, e l'emigrante Carlos García, che non nutriva simpatie per la sua patria, non esitò ad approfittare di quella convinzione e l'accentuó con un'avventura poco onorevole.[9] Morlini e Straparola erano pure al corrente della diceria; infatti stabiliscono come protagonista dei loro episodi, un ladro spagnolo. Il titolo della novela di Morlini suona: "De hispano qui decepit rusticum monachumque carmelitanum" e la conclusione "novela indicat hispanorum malitiam rusticorum superare," mentre che il titolo di Straparola dice: "Diego spagnolo compra gran quantità di galline da uno villano e dovendo fare il pagamento aggabba e il villano e un frate carmelitano." Oltre a quest'ultima avventura si nota ancora nell'opera di Carlos García, un altro episodio (187-194) che viene nella sua struttura, se non nella conclusione, dalla novela XX di Gerolamo Morlini (42).

Il debito dei romanzieri della picaresca verso la novellistica italiana appare ancor più accentuato nella narrazione di avventure completamente

---

[9]   Gli spagnoli erano già in quel tempo tacciati, senza ragioni plausibili, di condurre una vita disordinata, vagabonda e sfruttatrice. Perfino Francesco Guicciardini che si gloriava del suo acume storico ed analitico, cadde nella trappola denigratoria e tendenziosa che era comune tra gli europei del tempo e che creó poi la famigerata "leggenda negra." Notare la seguente citazione dello storico italiano estratta dai suoi *Viaies por España* (1512), riportata da Charles Gibson, pp. 34-35:" Indeed they (Gli spagnoli) are extremely avaricious and, since they lack the capacity to manufacture for themselves, they are skillfull at robbery. Formerly, when justice prevailed less in the kingdom than it does now, one encountered assassins everywhere...Their very astuteness make them good thieves...The Spaniard, because is more clever, surely robs better." Sugli stessi argomenti vedere anche gli articoli seguenti: Joaquín López-Barrera, "Libros raros y curiosos. Literatura hispanófoba en los siglos XVI y XVII," *Boletín de la Biblioteca Menéndez y Pelayo*, VII (1925), 83-95; 152-164; 379-395; VIII (1926), 137-149; IX (1927), 137-143.

estranee al filone principale. Qui il debito verso gli italiani è doppio: uno di struttura e l'altro di contenuto. Furono gli italiani, a cominciare da Boccaccio ad inventare o trarre dal folklore europeo, favole adatte a divertire i lettori oppressi dalle difficoltà e noie della vita di ogni giorno. Il gruppo dei giovani descritto nel *Decameron* s'allontana dal la peste fiorentina e si rifugia in un luogo isolato per raccontarsi giorno e notte avventure piacevoli, creando così per se stessi, una torre d'avorio invalicabile.

In alcuni romanzi picareschi, il protagonista, dopo essere passato attraverso avventure che hanno messo in pericolo la sua vita, per rifugiarsi in un mondo ideale e così cancellare ogni traccia del rischio trascorso, racconta avventure piacevoli e leggere che hanno l'unico fine di allontanare gli ascoltatori dall'atmosfera penosa in cui ha dovuto dibattersi. Mateo Alemán nel suo *Guzmán de Alfarache* usa abbondantemente questa tecnica distensiva ideata dai novellieri italiani (232-577). La storia di Ozmín e Daraja (273-295) è narrata nella geniale compagnia di religiosi, dopo che Guzmán e stato ingiustamente bastonato da guardie troppo zelanti. Il piacevole episodio di Dorido e Cloridia (375-382) è riferito attorno a una mensa imbandita al sapersi che Guzmán è stato cacciato dal servizio del cardinale romano. Sono narrate anche nella stessa atmosfera le avventure di Dorotea e Bonifacio (492-500), quando il povero Sayavedra, servo del Guzmán, perde il cervello e si getta dalla nave che riporta Guzmán in Italia, annegando.

Non solo è questa forma strutturale ricavata dai novellieri italiani, ma anche il contenuto stesso di alcuni episodi riecheggia di novelle e favole italiane. L'episodio di Dorotea e Bonifacio ha, per esempio, un precedente, negli *Hecatommithi* di Girald Cinthio (222-225). Molti altri romanzi considerati come picaresca minore, tra i quali s'incontra la produzione voluminosa di Alonso de Castillo Solórzano, seguono i modelli italiani sia nella struttura come nel contenuto.[10]

In conclusione, crediamo di poter dire che il romanzo picaresco spagnolo ha ricevuto influenze notevoli dal la letteratura italiana. Le influenze si estendono principalmente a due campi: 1 — Influenza ideologica. Le opere di Pulci e Folengo presentano figure letterarie della qualità di Margutte, Cingar, Fracassus e Falchetto che posseggono "in nuce" caratteristiche picaresche ben delineate. Questi anti-eroi non raggiungono però nella loro

---

[10]   Sarebbe pedante a questo punto mettere sossopra tutta la picaresca minore per scoprire le influenze italiane. Il lavoro comparativo fatto sembra sufficiente per nostro studio. Se si vogliono ulterior informazioni sulla influenza italiana nella picaresca minore, vedere Gustavo Alvaro, "El cuento intercalado en la novela picaresca," *Hispanófila*, 40, 1-8.

concezione della vita e visione della società le profondità ideologiche e l'attitudine disperata e tragica dei pícaros spagnoli. 2 — Influenza materiale. I romanzieri picareschi spagnoli copiarono nella loro totalità o in parte varie novelle italiane e le inserirono nelle loro narrazioni autobiografiche sia come avventure personal dei loro protagonisti sia come storie separate dal contesto generale del romanzo.

Southeastern Massachusetts University

OPERE CITATE

Alemán, Mateo. *Guzmán de Alfarache* in *La novela picaresca española*. Madrid: Aguilar, 1966.

Aretino, Pietro. *I Ragionamenti*. Roma: Frank, 1911.

Ariosto, Ludovico. *Orlando furioso*. Brescia: La Scuola, 1965.

Bandello, Matteo. *Le novelle*. Bari: Laterza, 1928.

Basile, Giovanni Battista. *Il Pentamerone*. New York: Liveright, 1927.

Boccaccio, Giovanni. *Decameron. Filocolo. Ameto. Fiammetta*. Milano: Ricciardi, 1953.

Croce, Benedetto. *Spagna nella vita italiana della Rinascenza*. Bari: Laterza, 1917.

Domenichi, Ludovico. *Sermoni et Facezie*. Vinegia: Giolitto de Ferrari, 1548.

Espinel, Vicente, *Marcos de Obregón* in La novela picaresca española. Ed. già citata.

Estelrich, Juan Luis. *Influencia de la lengua y la literatura italiana en la lengua y la literatura castellana*. Madrid: Fontanet, 1913.

Farinelli, Arturo. *Divagazioni erudite*. Torno: Bocca, 1925. *Italia e Spagna*. Torino: Bocca, 1929.

Fiorentino, Giovanni. *Il Pecorone*. Milano: Bompiani, 1944.

Folengo, Teofilo. *De Maccherone. Baldus*. Bari: Laterza, 1911.

Fucilla, Joseph. *Relaciones hispanoitalianas*. Madrid: Consejo superior de investigaciones científicas, 1953.

García, Carlos. *La desordenada codicia de los bienes agenos*. ed. Giulio Massano. Madrid: Porrúa, 1977,

García Berrio, Antonio. *España e Italia ante el conceptismo*. Madrid: Consejo superior de investigaciones científicas, 1968.

Gibson, Charles. *The Black Legend*. New York: Knopf, 1969.

Girald Cinthio, Giovanni B. *Hecatommithi ovvero cento novelle*. Venezia: Zopini, 1580.

Hernández, Jesús Helí. *Antecedentes literarios de la novela picaresca española.* Madrid: Porrúa, 1982.

Lazarillo de Tormes en *La novela picaresca española.* Ed. già citata.

Meozzi, Antero. *Azione e diffusione del la letteratura italiana in Europa (sec. XV-XVII)* Pisa: Valerini, 1932.

Morlini, Hieronimi. *Novellae. Fabulae. Comoedia.* Lutetiae Parisiorum: Jannet, 1855.

Pulci, Luigi. *Il Morgante.* Milano: Rizzoli, 1921.

Quevedo, Francisco. *La vida del Buscón* in *La novela picaresca española,* ed. già citata.

Ricapito, Joseph. *Toward a definition of the Picaresque.* (Ann Arbor: UP, 1964.)

Sacchetti, Franco. *Il trecentonovelle.* Torino: Einaudi, 1970.

Salernitano, Masuccio. *Il novellino.* Napoli: Morano, 1874.

Sansovino, Francesco. *Delle cento novelle.* Venetia: Rampazetto, 1563.

Sercambi, Giovanni. *Novelle.* Bari: Laterza, 1922.

Solórzano Castillo, Alonso de. *Aventuras del Bachiller Trapaza. La Garduña de Sevilla.* in *La novela picaresca española.* ed. già citata.

Straparola, Giovan Francesco. *Le piacevoli notti.* Bari: Laterza, 1927.

Boccaccio-Piccolomini-Rojas:
A Return to the Sources

Augustus A. Mastri

La Celestina has long been the object of study and commentary by many scholars from various backgrounds and with different points of view. The work presents many difficulties of interpretation, of authorship, of sources, to name just a few. It certainly is one of the best works from Spanish literature exemplifying a most vivid and profound relationship with the culture of Italy. This connection, of course, is most evident when we consider Rojas' work in terms of its literary sources, a question long discussed but hardly settled to everyone's satisfaction. Because of this, it might still be fruitful to review the most salient criticism on the relationship of *La Celestina* with Boccaccio's *L'elegia di Madonna Fiammetta* and Aeneas Sylvius Piccolomini's *The Tale of Two Lovers*, and to make a further comparison among the characters in the three works, showing how they are inextricably related and pointing to one clear conclusion. Whatever the authors' intentions, there is at least one tragic irony underlying all three works, namely, the sacrifice of a woman's life for a, more or less, unworthy lover.

Italian critical studies of *La Celestina* have been influential both in scope and in importance. Benedetto Croce, long the dominating figure of Italian scholarship, stated that it was useless to look for any kind of moral or immoral interpretation because the question was not applicable to *La Celestina* or to any other work of art and poetry, a view diametrically opposed to Bataillon's (*La Cèlestine*, 178 ff). Croce also remarked on the coherent nature of the work, thus rendering merely academic the question of the number of authors. He further showed his approval by defining *La Celestina* a classic which, "dà una nuova variazione di un canto che l'umanità non ha cessato mai e forse non cesserà mai di cantare, parla ancora a noi e lega la nostra attenzione e prende la nostra fantasia" (*Poesia*, 212).

Interestingly, a younger Italian scholar, Alberto del Monte, sides with the moralizing intent seen by Bataillon through a symbolic and novel-interpretation of three key elements, the garden, the ladder, and the night, leading to the conclusion that,

> Appare dunque lecito riconoscere una struttura tematico-simbolica, i cui elementi sono correlati e necessari: l'*huerto-paradisus*/l'*escala-ascensio*/la *noche-peccatum*. L'individualizzazione di tale simbologia conferma l'intenzione morale e il carattere esemplare della *Celestina*. (114)

This interpretation would explain (finally) that Calisto's death was not caused by a mere accident but by divine retribution.

In the philological sphere, Emma Scoles's study on the first Italian translation of *La Celestina* has received high praise, making it necessary to use it as a guide for any kind of textual study. On the study of style, Carmelo Samoá's work has prompted one critic to state that, "Lo que parece todavía hoy indiscutible es que, después del libro de Carmelo Samoná, no se ha escrito nada nuevo de valor sobre el estilo de *La Celestina*."[1]

Oddly, one of the earliest, most assiduous, and indefatigable scholars of Italo-Spanish literary relations, Arturo Farinelli, paid scant attention to our three works' meeting points. On *The Tale*'s influence, for instance, this scholar only mentions the letters and the deaths of the protagonists (*Italia e Spagna*, 232-34). The systematic study of *Fiammetta* and of *The Tale* viewed as sources of *La Celestina* had been launched, albeit within limits, by the distinguished Spanish scholar, M. Menéndez Pelayo, in 1910. Commenting on *The Tale*, he observes that, "Traducida u original, la había leido de seguro Fernando de Rojas, y no fue de los libros que menos huella dejaron en su espíritu y en su estilo" (336).

The analogies pointed out by him were, first of all, the argument of both stories, since both of them tell about the love and death of two young lovers, in which "se mezcla el placer con las lágrimas, y una siniestra fatalidad surge

---

[1] Leonor Piñero Ramirez, ("El hispanismo, 54). This article is, overall, very laudatory of Italian scholars' contributions to Celestina studies and gives an excellent synopsis of their works. See also Dean W. McPheeters, "The Present Status of *Celestina* Studies," Symposium, 12 (1958), where Samoá's work is called one of the worthiest ones of the 20th century.

en el seno mismo del deleite," although pointing out that the situation of the characters was different, since Piccolomini's book deals with adulterous love and its tragedy, belonging to the moral order, takes place not by external means but by burning passion. Other analogies believed by him to be significant were the name of Lucretia (strangely overlooking to mention Sosia's) and some passages of La Celestina, "Que inmediatamente recuerdan otros de Eurialo," such as the descriptions of the beauty of Melibea and Lucretia, and their respective meetings with a bawd (337-339). Believing the story to be "la interpretación estética de un suceso real acaecido en Siena," (337). Menéndez Pelayo opines that,

> En lo que la historia de Eurialo y Lucrecia pudo servir de modelo a la Celestina fue en la eloquencia patética de algunos trozos y en aquella especie de psicología afectiva y profunda que el culto, gentil y delicado espíritu de Eneas Silvio adivinó quizá el primero entre los modernos. (337)

The plausibility of The Tale's story is of secondary importance, but it ought to be kept in mind.[2]

As for the relationship to Fiammetta, in his opinion it was not as important as the one with The Tale but, he conceded,

> Pero es imposible dejar de reconocer en la retórica sentimental de la obra (La Celestina), en las apostrofes y exclamaciones patéticas, al lector asiduo de la Fiameta, que fue el tipo de todas las novelas amatorias de nuestro siglo XV. (350-351)

The critic concluded his brief references to Boccaccio's work returning to The Tale's greater importance, stating that the interminable monologues of Fiammetta was a lesson for Rojas, who generally preferred "el arte de suaves matices y el fino proceso psicológico de Eneas Silvio," although "se inclinó más bien en las últimas escenas a la manera vehemente y ampulosa de la Fiammetta" (351).

However, F. Castro Guisasola later presented some well grounded objections to Menéndez Pelayo's preference of Piccolomini as a more significant source for La Celestina, than Boccaccio, but, unfortunately, went to the other extreme. In his very ambitious work, Observaciones sobre las fuentes

---

[2] On this question it would be very helpful to read Frugoni's article.

literatias de 'La Celestina,' he claimed that the similarities pointed out by Menéndez Pelayo were purely casual, since they could be found in other works. Also, the name of Lucretia had very little significance, the same as with the similarity of the physical appearance of Melibea and Lucretia, since almost identical descriptions were contained in *Tristán de Leonis*, in *Corvacho*, and other works. And at last, and most important, for this critic not even the general argument of *The Tale* had much significance, not only because, "Historias de amor y muerte de dos jóvenes amantes" were present in any age and literature but also because in *The Tale* Lucretia was the only one to die, while Euryalus consoled himself when the Emperor wedded him to a maiden of ducal rank, most beautiful, and chaste, and virtuous" (*The Tale*, 135). So that Castro Guisasola concluded with the statement ". . . no creo probada definitivamente la influencia directa del *Euríalo (146)*.

On the other hand, the author of *Observaciones* not only agreed with Menéndez Pelayo that the last scenes of *La Celestina* reflected "La retórica sentimental y patética y la manera vehemente y ampulosa de la *Fiameta*," but also pointed out that there were other more tangible examples reminiscent of Boccaccio.

Foremost among these examples are the scenes referring to the suicide of Melibea and the attempted suicide of *Fiammetta*. Just before her attempt, Fiammetta, as usual, gives a soliloquy, while Melibea recites a monologue. According to Castro Guisasola's interpretation, Fiammetta's soliloquy is:

> Parecido hasta en las ideas al monólogo de Melibea, sola ya en la torre, y a las palabras que dirije a su padre antes de despeñarse. Si algo valiera mi modesta opinión, yo diría que este pasaje de la *Fiameta*, fuente indudable de Rojas es el que sugirió la catástrofe de Melibea. (16)

As Menéndez Pelayo did with Piccolomini so Castro Guisasola did with this particular point by exaggerating it so much.

To be sure, the circumstances are very similar. For instance, the method chosen for the suicide is the same. Fiammetta intends to jump "dall'alto palagio" while Melibea kills herself by jumping off the "azotea alta" and not, say, by taking poison. Another common characteristic is that both women use a stratagem in order to be left alone to carry out their designs. On her part, Fiammetta tries to get rid of the nurse by saying that the old woman's talk has had an effect on her and that now she wants her to leave because she has become sleepy. She says,

Ecco, carissima madre, li tuoi parlari verissimi con utile frutto luogo nel petto mio hanno trovato, ma acció che'l cieco furore esca dalla pazza anima, alquanto di qui ti cessa, e me di dormire disidirosa al sonno lascia. (131)

On her part, Melibea first sends her father off by telling him she wishes to go on the roof to enjoy the "deleitosa vista de los navíos," adding slyly,

Mas, si a ti placerá, padre mío, mandar traer algún instrumento de cuerdas, con que sufra mi dolor o tañendo o cantando; de manera que, aunque aqueje por una parte la fuerza de su accidente, mitigarlo han por otra los dulces sones y alegre armonía. (202)

Then, she gets rid of the nurse by telling her, even more cunningly, since she is no longer addressing her trusting and unaware father,

Lucrecia, amiga mía, muy alto es esto. Ya me pasa por dejar la compañía de mi padre. Baja a él y dile que se pare al pie desta torre, que le quiero decir una palabra que se me olvidó que hablase a mi madre. (202)

With all this, however, in spite of what Castro Guisasola says, the two talks are not very similar at all. Fiammetta promises herself vengeance on her rival, "Oggi comincerai le vendette della nemica donna" (132). Then asks the gods something which to her is very important, but not to Melibea, namely, that her death be not considered infamous. She invokes, for the umpteenth time, her gods, "Ma, o iddii, se in voi niuna pietá si truova, negli ultimi miei prieghi siatemi graziosi: fate la mia morte senza infamia passare tra le genti" (132). And in order for this to happen she is forced to die without telling anyone the reason, "muoio senza osare manifestare la cagione," while Melibea tells her father everything just before she makes the fatal jump. (203-205)

The feelings which the two women have about the afterlife are also very importantly dissimilar. Fiammetta prays to Mercury to find her a comfortable place for her soul in the other world, while Melibea does not have any doubt about her being able to join her dead lover, as shown by when she says, "Así, contentarle he en la muerte, pues no tuve tiempo en la vida . . . . Espérame, ya voy" (205). More dissimilarities about the suicide could be mentioned, but

99

it should be obvious to see that Castro Guisasola's over-zealousness to correct Menéndez Pelayo sent him also off the track.

María Rosa Lida de Malkiel, however, seems to be a much more cautious and thorough critic, at least on this particular topic, than either Menéndez Pelayo or Castro Guisasola. In the part of her impressive masterwork dealing with the antecedents of the characters she is the first one to point out the obvious relationship between the personality of Fiammetta and that of Calisto, thus reinforcing the case for Boccaccio's contribution. And as for the importance of Piccolomini's work she says, "A mi ver, la *Historia* ejerció en la *Tragicomedia* una influencia no escusa, aunque totalmente negativa, en el carácter de los enamorados y en algunas escenas en que intervienen" (*Antecedentes*, 389-390). The phrase "aunque totalmente negativa" is the objectionable part of the statement because there is also a *positive*, and very important, influence between the two works. And along the same lines a further objection must be raised to this critic's statement that, "El contraste (between *La Celestina* and *The Tale*) *es a veces tan riguroso que dificilmente podrá achacarse al azar. No puede haber, por ejemplo, mayor oposición que la que existe entre los dos héroes.*"[3] The distinguished critic brings much evidence to support the above conclusions but there is also ample evidence that Calisto and Euryalus *do* have things in common. Moreover, and this is what this writer considers most important, she fails to point out the most important factor in the understanding of the "tragic comedy," and that is that even though the two characters, Calisto and Euryalus, might be very different in their ways of acting, they have one most important thing in common: In spite of their noble lineages both of them are dislikable, although Euryalus more so than Calisto. Their role in their two respective works is to show the tragic irony of the condition in which the two female characters end up. Giving themselves completely to unworthy lovers, they doom themselves to a tragic end. This must be so in order for *La Celestina* not to be a morality play because, in order to have been effectively moralizing, the author would have logically set up *two*, not one, worthy characters and then shown the effect of the wrath of God, or whatever else, on them as punishment of their sinful actions. María Rosa Lida is correct in observing that the author of *La Celestina* borrowed and juggled various elements from *Fiammetta* and *The Tale*, but in her zeal of magnifying the originality of *La*

---

[3] *Originalidad*, 390. The parentheses and the underlining are mine. This author's references to *Fiammetta* and *De duobus amantibus* are scattered throughout the massive tome, but mainly on pp. 386-392 and 445-451.

Celestina she lessens the importance of the Italians' influence. A further look at the problem seems warranted.

In an effort to discuss more clearly the play of interrelationships we need primarily to look at the characters, keeping in mind the following outline:

1.   Fiammetta's influence on characterization of Calisto
2.   Fiametta's influence on characterization of Melibea
3.   Lucretia's influence on characterization of Melibea
4.   Eurialo's influence on characterization of Calisto[4]

1.   The basic influence of Fiammetta on Calisto is that the author gives him some of her features, which, although forgivable in a woman, would make a man, to say the least, not worthy of admiration. Some of these features include a sense of inability to act, hopelessness, lack of free, strong will. From the start Fiammetta gives this impression when she describes her reaction to having become a prisoner of love,

> Quivi, poi che nella mia camera sola e oziosa mi ritrovai, da diversi disii accesa e piena di nuovi pensieri, e da molte sollecitudini stimolata, ogni fine di quelli nella immaginata effigie dal piaciuto giovane terminado . . . (*Fiammetta*, 13).

This sets the tone of her seemingly interminable litany of self-pitying remarks.

The same sentiment and reaction are shown by Calisto with his morose retreats in his room, dreaming and talking about the object of his love, as shown by Sempronio's answer to Pármeno about the activity of their "desesperado" master. He says,

> Alli está tendido en el estrado, cabe la cama, donde le dejaste anoche: que ni ha dormido ni está despierto. Si alla entró, ronca; si me salgo, canta o devanea. No le tomo tiento si con aquello pena o descaunsa (117).

Their private rooms serve for them as refugees against any kind of emo-

---

[4]   Panfilo is really of no relevance to this discussion, since he only exists in Fiammetta's mind and is known only through her words. But it must be remembered, though, that he is a faithless and unworthy lover, who abandons Fiammetta in spite of all his pledges and oaths (38 ff., but especially p. 42).

tional unsettling from the outside world. For instance, when she hears a merchant saying that Panfilo is married to another woman she shows how she can become violently enraptured in her passion and inner conflict and then escape to her room, where she can continue self analysis, as returning to the womb, "Io con anima piena d'angosciosa ira, non altramente fremendo che il lione libico . . . entrata nella mia camera, amaramente cominciai a piangere (*Fiammetta*, 65).

A corresponding reaction can be seen in Calisto, as when he learns about his servants' deaths. He should immediately go out and do something about it but instead, going into a lengthy monologue, he puts it off. "Mañana," he says, "haré que vengo de fuera si pudiera vengar estas muertes" (165). But at the same time he rationalizes about their deaths by saying, "Ellos eran sobrados y esforzados: ahora o en otro tiempo de pagar habían" (165). This example of Calisto's rationalization also reflects a certain egotism and self centeredness which are probably the two most important elements borrowed by Rojas from Fiammetta and given to his male protagonist. He does not care very much about their deaths and Celestina's because they are no longer needed. He says about it, "Que más me va en conseguir la ganancia de la gloria que espero, que en la pérdida de morir los que murieron" (165). This same egotism is reflected by Fiammetta when she wishes the death of Panfilo's father, who is calling his son away from her. She says on one occasion, "Cosí come, tu non con lui, lungamente é vivuto, se gli piace, per innanzi si viva, e se non, muoiasi" (*Fiammetta*, 36). And again she says, later on,

> . . . io priego sovente per la sua morte, fermamente credendo lui cagione della tua dimora; e se cosí non e, almeno del tôrmiti pur fu. Ma io non dubito che, della morte pregando, non gli si prolunghi la vita, tanto mi sono gl'iddii contrarii e male esaudevoli in ogni cosa. (75)

Fiammetta's sentimental weakness and pleasure in feeling sorry for herself finds outlet in her tears, in her closed room, and we might expect Calisto to do the same, for he asks Sempronio, "No sabes que alivia la pena llorar la causa? Cuánto es dulce a los tristes quejar su pasión? Cuánto relieven y disminuyen los lagrimosos gemidos el dolor?" (55).

At this point one must wonder, why does Rojas give Calisto such an unattractive personality? We suggest a twofold answer. Rojas purposely wants his male protagonist to be unworthy of the reader's admiration or empathy so as to make Melibea's situation more poignant, more tragic. Since Fiammetta is a less attractive, more boring personality than Melibea, Calisto's identification with the weak Fiammetta will make him appear doubly the worse.

2. Fiammetta, from a position of a seemingly experienced woman of the world, involved in all sorts of social and recreational functions, becomes a tiresome bore. Her growth, if there is any, is in retrospective. She lacks natural expression. Her feelings are investigated either psychologically or through literary, somewhat stilted memories. Her love is mainly mental, not physical. She confesses,

> Certo, se questa fosse la cagione per la quale io l'amassi (physical attraction and pleasure) . . . ma in ció mi sia Iddio testimonio che cotale accidente fin ed é cagione menomissima dell'amore che io gli porto. (28)

On the other hand, Melibea's love becomes totally fulfilled in all of its possibilities. Melibea's love is real, tangible, mental, physical, and enjoyable once it has flourished and become fulfilled during the month-long nightly visits. With Fiammetta it had been but a flash, nearly over as fast as it had started. "Amore il primo dí di me ebbe interissima possessione" (13), but soon the object of her love becomes only a memory. As Stephen Gilman points out, in Fiammetta, "There is nothing comparable to that slow growth to ardor in Melibea" (*The Art*, 251). Fiammetta's suffering is convincing enough, but one is doubtful about whether she had been capable of experiencing with Panfilo the satisfying "gozo" and "deleyte" Melibea achieves. Boccaccio's heroine's nostaligic recollection of her past enjoyments with her lover might be sincerely and evocatively expressed but, because of her insistence on them, the reader begins to wonder how much of it is true. This is evident even in one of the most beautifully nostalgic passages describing how familiar places of past happiness rekindle in her a burning passion.

> Il ricordarmi quivi molte volte essere stata da Panfilo accompagnata, amore e dolore, vedendomivi senza esso, senza dubbio nessuno mi cresceva. So non vedea né monte né valle alcuna . . . non conoscessi per testimonio e delle mie e delle sue allegrezze essere stata. Niuno lito, né scoglio, né isoletta ancora si vedea, che io non dicessi: 'Qui fui io con Panfilo, e cosí mi disse, e cosí quivi facemmo'. (80)

Fiammetta's and Calisto's undecisiveness contrasts sharply with Melibea's straightforward resolve. This is nowhere else shown better than in the suicide episodes, where Fiammetta is incapable of carrying out her intention. Her repeated comparisons of herself to mythological characters betray an enormous amount of self-love, which prevents her from achieving through death the union with her loved one, as she had foreseen in her suicidal deliberations, when, convinced of the impossibility of Panfilo's return and of her leaving her husband and family, to seek her loved one, she decides to take a chance on the possibility of joining him with her spirit, free of her body.

> E se agli spiriti sciolti dalla corporal carcere e al nuovo mondo è alcuna libertá, senza alcuno indugio con lui mi ricongiugneró, e dove il corpo mio esser non puote, l'anima vi stará in quella vece. Ecco, adungue morrò. (129)

But Fiammetta's attempt is ineffectual. More than her nurse, it is she who in the end talks herself out of jumping to her death. Not so with Melibea. Her decision is immediate and the execution is swift, as if Rojas purposely wanted to avoid the lessening or even complete disappearance of the tragic effect. In connection with the suicide, the parallels between the two heroines is not just the method chosen, but the reason for it, that is, the possibility of joining in spirit the loved one. Among her final words, Melibea justifies what she is about to do by saying, "Su muerte convida a la mía, convídame y fuerza que sea presto sin dilación, muéstrame que ha de ser despeñada, por seguirle en todo" (205). Unlike Fiammetta, however, Melibea has truly experienced love, she has given her body and soul to Calisto and, therefore her suicide, after his death, becomes inevitable.

3.   Even though the relationship between Lucretia and Euryalus, being adulterous, cannot be exactly matched up with the one between Melibea and Calisto, there is definitely an influence of the characterization of Lucretia on Melibea. Fiammetta's influence, regarding Melibea, is mostly one of contrast, while that of Lucretia is a somewhat more direct one. It is the realism of Lucretia's character which is more importantly related to Melibea than anything else. Besides the similarity of their physical attributes, they have in common the forcefulness to take charge of their lives and make a total commitment to their lovers. Therein lies the tragedy. Lucretia, as an adulteress, is certainly more sinful, more devious than Melibea, but not more sincere in her consuming love. Lucretia's words about giving herself to her lover are proven

to be true indeed, since, as with Melibea, she also experiences a "slow growth to order," as is apparent from a letter written by her early on in the affair, in which she cautions Euryalus,

> So far, all's well. If you think you will desert me, say so, before my love burns higher. Let us not begin what later we'll repent of. In all things, we should look to the end. . . . For now I give myself to you, and pledge my faith. But I'll not begin to be yours, unless I am to be for ever yours. (46)

"For ever," with no equivocations, just as with Melibea. And although the means are different, the two heroines come to "the end" because of the loss of the object of their existence.

The above quote shows Lucretia to be quite a mature and level-headed young woman, with some experience behind her. In contrast, Melibea is still original, but she also is quite capable of running the household. Unlike Fiammetta's, Lucretia's love is emotionally and physically fulfilling and, at the same time, consuming, just as Melibea's.

Much has already been said about the similarity of parallels of Lucretia's physical description to Melibea's and about the two heroines' similar angry reaction to the bawd. In the latter case, however, there is a distinction to be made. Lucretia's reaction is entirely pretense, a show put on exclusively because of her concern about being seen with such a disreputable character, lest her reputation suffer (28-30). Inwardly, though, she is immensely pleased, as the bawd imagines (29). Melibea's reaction, on the other hand, seems to be a more honest one (75-88), since Celestina's views it as an obstacle, however useless, to surpass," Más fuerte estaba Troya, y aun otras más bravas he yo amansado!" (76). It is obvious that Rojas has made of Melibea a character much more admirable than her two counterparts, with her honesty evident in other occasions, such as when she rejects the idea of marriage by declaring, "Más vale ser buena amiga que mala casada. . . . No quiero marido, no quiero ensuciar los nudos del matrimonio" (182). But, as Lucretia and Fiammetta, she too is a victim of a lesser individual.

4.   Contrary to María Rosa Lida de Malkiel's conclusions (390-91), Calisto is a kindred spirit of Euryalus, only younger and less experienced. With time and opportunity he too would likely become a cynical exploiter of women. It is difficult to find anything admirable in either of these two protagonists, except, perhaps, Euryalus' ability to learn Italian in the shortest time imaginable. He is a nobleman at Sigismund's court, but his actions are less than flattering,

if not downright cowardly, as when he is fearful of discovery, "Terrified at this, Euryalus felt faint and promptly began to hate Lucretia, saying to himself: 'Dolt that I am! . . . now I will be made a laughingstock, and lose the Emperor's friendship. His friendship? I'll be lucky if I keep my life. Who can save me from this? I'm bound to die" (64-65). It is not just his words which diminish him, but also his hiding under the bed. All of his professions of love (37, 40, 54, etc.) are shown their true worth when he curses both love and the wiles of women,

> What are the joys of love, if they are bought so dear? Its pleasure is short, and very long in sorrow. . . . We'll not put up with briefest labour for ever-lasting joy, but for love, whose happiness may be compared to smoke. . . . Lucretia never loved me, but wished to catch me. . . . Often had I heard of the wiles of women, and knew not how to avoid them. But if this time I escape, no woman's tricks shall ever deceive me. (65-66)

Lucretia's cunning saves him, but his recidivism is established, for on other occasions he reacts in similarly ignoble fashion (74, 90-91, 117). He equates love with the sexual act and he cares more about his honor and reputation that about Lucretia. He is sorrowful at Lucretia's death, but he is consoled by his marriage to "a maiden of ducal rank, most beautiful, and chaste, and virtuous" (135).

Calisto is cut from similar cloth. The sincerity of his real love, as opposed to physical love, is put in a dubious light by his servants mocking comments to him and about him (31, 53, 54, 168). His valor is tested when he is confronted by the servants' death (165), where he chooses to stay inside and pretend he is away. But most of all, it is his ignoble, even ridiculous death that puts him at a par with Euryalus. There is nobility in Melibea's comportment but not in the noble Euryalus and Calisto.

As Fiammetta, to a lesser extent, had become a victim of an unworthy lover, so has been Lucretia and so now is Melibea. Rojas, availing himself of Boccaccio and Piccolomini's character portrayals, creates in Melibea a protagonist who is not only tragic but real.

University of Louisville

WORKS CITED

Bataillon, Marcel. *La Celestine selon Fernando de Rojas*. Paris: Didier, 1961.

Boccaccio, Giovanni. *L'elegia di Madonna Fiammetta*. Bari: Laterza, 1939.

Croce, Benedetto. *Poesia antica e moderna*. 2nd ed. Bari: Laterza, 1943, 209-222.

Farinelli, Arturo. *Italia e Spagna*. I. Torino: Bocca, 1929.

Frugoni, A. "Enea Silvio Piccolomini e l'avventura senese di Gaspare Schlick," *Rinascita*, 4 (1941), 229-49.

Gilman, Stephen. *The Art of La Celestina*. Madison: The U. of Wisconsin Press, 1956.

Guisasola, F. Castro. *Observaciones sobre las fuentes literarias de La Celestina*. Madrid, 1924.

Malkiel, María Rosa Lide de. *La originalidad artística de "La Celestina"*. Buenos Aires: Editorial universitaria de Buenos Aires, 1960.

Menéndez Pelayo, Marcelino. *Orígenes de la novela*. III. Buenos Aires: Emecé editores, 1945.

Piccolomini, Aeneas Sylvius. (Pius II). *The Tale of Two Lovers*. Trans. Flora Grierson. New York: Richard R. Smith Inc., 1930.

Ramirez, Leonor Piñero. "El hispanismo italiano y *La Celestina*." *Revista de filología de la universidad de La Laguna*, 3 (1984), 47-60.

Rojas, Fernando de. *La Celestina*. New York: Las Americas Pub. Co., 1967.

Samoná, Carmelo. *Aspetti del retoricismo nella "Celestina."* Roma: Studi di letteratura spagnola (Facoltá di Magistero dell'Università di Roma), 1954.

Scoles, Emma. "Note sulla prima traduzione italiana della *Celestina*." Studi Romanzi, 33 (1961), 153-217.

Cervantes e Pirandello

Giacomo Striuli

Cervantes nacque nel 1547 e morì il 23 Aprile 1616, dieci giorni dopo la scomparsa di William Shakespeare. Il destino ha stranamente accomunato nella morte due scrittori che ci hanno dato un archetipo universale che supera tutte le barriere nazionali, culturali e linguistiche: Don Quijote e Amleto. Per noi moderni, queste due immagini dell'eroe folle rispecchiano la nostra realtà interiore, sono l'incarnazione dell'individuo che vive oggi in una società alienata e alienante. Scopo di questa disamina è quello di valutare l'incidenza dell'archetipo cervantino sulla poetica di Luigi Pirandello (1867-1936).

È indubbio che Cervantes sia lo scrittore che ha maggiormente influenzato la letteratura italiana. La prima parte del suo capolavoro, *El Quijote*, apparve nel 1605, la seconda nel 1615. Il romanzo fu tradotto in italiano da Bartolomeo Gamba nel 1818, ma era già stato imitato da molti sia nell'originale che nella versione francese. Tra i grandi scrittori dell'ottocento, si è maggiormente notato l'influsso del *Don Chisciotte* sull'Alfieri, sul Leopardi, e soprattutto sul Manzoni.[1] Ma già Giovanni Getto ha esauerientemente discusso le affinità tra Don Chisciotte, Don Ferrante e le loro rispettive biblioteche.

El Quijote anticipa molte tecniche e strategie che sono al centro della narratologia moderna. Già in nuce troviamo, nel testo cervantino, quella obliterazione del divario tra testo e lettore che è al centro delle teorie di Umberto Eco (1932-   ). E infatti, Don Quijote, diventando lettore di sè stesso, partecipa attivamente alla significazione del testo letterario. Sarebbe interessante trattare l'influenza dell'archetipo donchisciottesco su scrittori

---

[1] Si veda Alda Croce in *Letterature comparate*.1

come Italo Cavino (1913-1985) e Leonardo Sciascia (1921-   ), ma la trattazione diventerebbe troppo lunga e complessa. Mi limiterò soltanto a mettere evidenza le somiglianze tra il capolavoro cervantino, *El Quijote*, e il saggio sull' *Umorismo* (1908), summa del pensiero pirandelliano. Anche se distanti fra loro nel tempo e nello spazio, c'è un denominatore comune che accomuna Cervantes a Pirandello: l'uso dell'umorismo e del teatro per rappresentare le dialettiche arte/vita, illusione/realtà.

Il grande critico cervantino Americo Castro, pur mettendo in risalto le affinità tra i due scrittori (la comunanza di certi moduli narrativi per colmare il divario arte/vita, per esempio, "il teatro nel teatro"), non dà grande rilevanza alla presenza di tecniche cervantine in pirandello, attribuendole a un fenomeno di assimilazione culturale che si manifesta in molti scrittori moderni.[2] Gaetano Cipolla mette in risalto la presenza cervantina nel saggio sull'*Umorismo* attraverso la mediazione del poema "Don Chisciotti" di Giovanni Meli (1740-1815).[3]

Sia per Cervantes che per Pirandello, il teatro e la narrativa sono un gioco di specchi, un medium artistico di cui si avvale lo scrittore per dar forma all'illusorietà del reale. I personaggi pirandelliani al pari di Don Quijote sono consapevoli della loro realtà fittizia.[4] Nel romanzo cervantino Don Quijote diventa lettore di se stesso quando scopre l'esistenza del manoscritto apocrifo di Cide Hamete Benenjeli. Se è il libro ciò che dà consistenza al suo essere, vuol dire che il suo destino è confinato al limite temporale che lo scrittore ha imposto alla sua storia. Il libro dentro il libro è la realtà medesima. Abbiamo così una variante del la "myse en abyme" dantesca (il libro "galeotto" di Paolo e Francesca) o quella shakespeariana (il "play-within-the-play" in Amleto).[5] Lo stesso avviene nei drammi pirandelliani, basterà pensare ai *Sei personaggi in cerca d'autore* (1922). Don Quijote anticipa così quella problematica che sarà al centro del dramma pirandelliano (pensiamo al *Il fu Mattia Pascal*, 1904): non si può esistere senza un'identità. E finalmente, altro nesso rilevante è il concetto della follia quale specchio della frammentazione psicologica che obbliga l'individuo ad assumere ruoli cui deve assoggettarsi.

---

[2] Si veda Américo Castro, "Cervantes y Pirandelo."

[3] Secondo Cipolla, Pirandello e Meli, essendo entrambi siciliani, non sono solo strettamente vincolati da legami linguistici e culturali, ma anche da "a comon attitude toward the world and toward writing which can be summed up in one word: "Umorismo" (116).

[4] Per una discussione storica delle affinità cervantina si veda Giovanni Getto.

[5] Una microstoria che rispecchia la storia maggiore, cfr. Ricardou che sviluppa il concetto sulla base del termine proposto da André Gide. Nella prospettiva semiologica dei "personaggi di carta" si veda anche Roland Barthes in *L'analisi del racconto*.

Nel saggio sull'*Umorismo* Pirandello si avvale della vita e dell'opera di Cervantes per veicolare la sua poetica. Lo scrittore siciliano si serve del contrasto tra Ariosto e Cervantes per sottolineare la differenza tra "ironia" e "umorismo". Mentre l'"ironista", quale Ariosto, si mantiene sempre distaccato dalla sua creazione artistica, e addirittura ride delle folli avventure dei suoi protagonisti mostrando anche nei momenti di maggior tensione "di aver coscienza della irrealtà di quel mondo fantastico" (96), Cervantes, il vero "umorista", si identifica con i suoi personaggi. Lo scrittore spagnolo pertanto riesce a creare un personaggio per cui tutto è naturale, completamente capace di accettare il favoloso con la massima naturalezza. Don Quijote, dice Pirandello, "non finge di credere come fa l'Ariosto, quel mondo meraviglioso delle leggende cavalleresche: ci crede sul serio; lo porta dentro, lo ha in sé quel mondo, che è la sua realtà, la sua ragion d'essere' (97). Per Don Quijote i molini a vento sono molini a vento, non pensa che siano il frutto della sua follia. Egli è convinto che sia stato il mago Freston a trasformarli per incantesimo in giganti: "ecco la leggenda nella realtà vivente" (97). Detto questo, Pirandello sembra già anticipare il profondo influsso che il "real meravilloso" degli scrittori latino americani avrebbe avuto sulla letteratura contemporanea (pensiamo a Márquez, Asturias e Carpentier).

I continui riferimenti alla vita e all'opera di Cervantes nel saggio sull'*Umorismo* non solo dimostrano una attenta e approfondita lettura del *Quijote*, essi esprimono anche una sentita ammirazione per lo scrittore spagnolo. Pirandello colloca Cervantes ai vertici dell'arte umoristica al di sopra dei grandi "umoristi" italiani, quali Macchiavelli, Giordano Bruno e Manzoni; quest'ultimo è il solo che sembri uguagliare Cervantes. Scrive Pirandello: "così avviene che noi dovremmo tutti provar disprezzo e indignazione per Don Abbondio, per esempio, e stimar ridicolissimo e spesso un matto da legare Don Quijote; eppure siamo indotti al compatimento, finanche alla simpatia per quello, e ad ammirare con infinita tenerezza le ridicolaggini di questo nobilitate da un ideale così alto e puro" (139).

È certo che la follia è l'affinità fondamentale tra Pirandello e Cervantes. Essa e il perno attorno al quale ruota tutta la vicenda del romanzo cervantino, e costituisce il centro della poetica pirandelliana. La fuga verso un falso io non esiste, come non esiste l'autenticità. L'unica via d'uscita dal proprio stato di alienazione tanto nel *Quijote* quanto nei drammi pirandelliani è la morte o la follia. Non si può fare a meno di constatare che il tema della follia evidenzia il continuum letterario che avvicina la letteratura cavalleresca rinascimentale alla cosidetta letteratura della nevrosi di autori moderni che sono stati influenzati, nel nostro Paese, da Pirandello, Svevo, e Tozzi.

Eppure, anche se la follia e il nesso che unisce Ariosto, Cervantes e Pirandello, permangono differenze fondamentali nella trattazione che ne fanno i tre scrittori. Per esempio, sappiamo che Orlando e l'antecedente letterario di Don Quijote, ma l'eroe ariostesco impazzisce per amore, non per libri. La follia scoppia nel cervello di Orlando quando un pastore innocentemente gli racconta la storia d'amore tra due suoi ospiti, la bella Angelica, di cui il paladino è innamorato, e il fante saraceno, Medoro, suo mortale nemico. Denudatosi, Orlando nei tre mesi successivi sfoga la sua folle rabbia contro tutto e tutti. Sradica alberi, ammazza mani uomini e bestie con le sole mani. Il senno glielo riporterà dalla luna il cugino Astolfo dopo un viaggio miracoloso.

La follia di Don Quijote, invece, non è di origine amorosa, bensì libresca. Sono le eccessive letture dei poemi cavallereschi che lo portano alla pazzia. Nel primo capitolo impariamo che Don Quijote è nella realtà biografica Alonso Quijano el Bueno, un nobile decaduto, cinquantenne, celibe, alto, rinsecchito, solitario, e un po' filosofo. Parla il narratore: "En resolución, él se enfracasó tanto su lectura, que se le pasaban las noches leyendo de claro en claro, y los días de turbio en turbio; y así, del poco dormir y del mucho leer se le secó el cerebro de manera que vino a perder el juicio" (I.1). La follia si manifesta in una fortissima febbre che riduce il povero Alonso allo stato di un "mummia": "Visitáronle, en fin, y halláronle sentado en la cama, vestida una almilla de bayeta verde, con un bonete colorado toledano, y estaba tan seco y amojado, que no parecía sino hecho de carne momia (I). Una volta folle, Don Quijote continuerà a oscillare tra opposte condizioni psicologiche di insanità e di piena lucidità mentale: "Preguntó don Diego a su hijo qué había sacado en limpio del ingenio del huesped. A lo que él respondió: No le sacarán del borrador de su locura cuantos médicos y buenos escribanos tiene el mundo: él es un entreverado loco, lleno de lúcidos intervalos" (II, 18).

Impazzito, Alonso annuncia alla nipote e alla domestica che vuole diventare cavaliere errante. La sua decisione è irrevocabile. Don Quijote è certo che i romanzi cavallereschi gli daranno tutte le informazioni necessarie per attuare il suo proposito. Tralascia pertanto tutte le sue attività, perfino la caccia, che tanto lo appassionava. A nulla vale l'intervento dei suoi pochi amici, un prete e il barbiere, soli notabili della Mancha. Dedica un'intera settimana a restaurare l'armatura del trisavolo. Volendo essere degno del suo nuovo ruolo decide di dare un nome altisonante al suo malandato cavallo, che d'ora in poi si chiamerà Ronzinante. Per sè sceglie il nome di Don Quijote. E dato che un vero cavaliere non può essere tale senza la compagnia di una dama dal cuore puro, una povera contadina a lui del tutto sconosciuta, Aldonza Lorenza, diventa, nella sua fantasia, l'amatissima Dulcinea del Toboso. Gli eroi cavallereschi impazziscono per amore, e così decide di farlo anche Don Chisciotte di modo che egli possa emulare Orlando, il suo eroe. Sancio potrà poi riferire le sue pene d'amore all'amata Dulcinea. Semplici oggetti, quali la catinella del barbiere e i mulini a vento, si trasformano rispettivamente nell'elmo incantato di Mambrino e in minacciosi giganti: cose meravigliose, degne di essere lette in un romanzo cavalleresco. Evidentemente, per Don Chisciotte, non esiste distinzione tra il reale e l'immaginario.

La follia di Don Quijote rispecchia fedelmente l'eziologia patogena medievale. Sappiamo infatti che Cervantes, essendo figlio di un "chirurgo" che non doveva godere di grande popolarità, a giudicare dai suoi continui spostamenti, doveva ben intendersi dei sintomi clinici della pazzia. Don Quijote manifesta tutti i sintomi della nevrosi secentesca, e più precisamente, l'eziologia psicogena del "collerico". Ne abbiamo conferma leggendo gli scritti dei grandi umanisti coevi a Cervantes. Alfonso Martinez de Toledo, Arciprete di Talavera, per esempio, in *Corbacho* (1498), sembra riferirsi Don Quijote quando scrive che "hombres coléricos" sono "calientes y secos, por cuanto el elemento del fuego es su correspondiente, que es caliente y seco". Non solo gli attributi fisici di Don Quijote come per esempio, l'impetuosità e la magrezza, "animosos de corazón, ligeros por su cuerpo", ma anche le caratteristiche psicologiche come l'ingegno, "mucho sabios, sutiles e ingeniosos, muy solícitos y despachados" e l'amore per la giustizia confermano il ritratto clinico del collerico resoci da Martínez. In un'opera datata 1538, *De anima et vita*, Luis Vives spiega che l'eccesso di umore collerico genera la follia perchè altera la capacita del cervello di valutare le immagini che gli vengono trasmesse attraverso la vista: "La función imaginativa en el alma hace las veces de los ojos en el cuerpo, a saber: reciben imágenes mediante la vista, y hay una especie de vaso con abertura que le conserva; la fantasia, finalmente, reúne y separa aquellos datos que aislados y simples, recibiera la imaginación". Come scrive P.E. Russell, ragguardevole studioso cervantino, lo scrittore spagnolo avrebbe intenzionalmente sfruttato la malattia di un nevrotico a fini comici, onde cattivarsi la simpatia del lettore secenteso che avrebbe riso di gusto leggendo le azioni folli del povero Don Quijote.

La nozione che esiste un nesso inscindibile tra follia e umorismo è, dunque, il vincolo che accomuna maggiormente Pirandello a Cervantes. In apertura del saggio, nel tentativo di "storicizzare" la sua definizione di "umorismo", Pirandello si rifà appunto alla tradizione medievale degli "umori" allo scopo di radicare la sua nozione di "umorismo" in un contesto latino, e, di conseguenza, italiano. Pirandello rifiuta l'accezione inglese di "humour" quale "comicità". Con questo obbiettivo in mente, Pirandello si ricollega alla nozione medievale dei "quattro umori" citando i classici. Pirandello spiega che in origine la parola "umore" significava, "in senso materiale", corpo fluido, liquore, umidità o vapore, e, "in senso spirituale", fantasia, capriccio o vigore. In ogni caso, osserva lo scrittore, il termine "umorismo" in antichità era ritenuto "segno o cagione di malattia". A conferma di ciò, Pirandello cita Brunetto Latini: "Malinconia è un umore, che molti chiamano collera nera, ed è fredda, e secca, ed ha il suo sedio nello spino" (18). L'importanza di ciò si capisce nella seconda parte del saggio la dove Pirandello enuclea più compiutamente la sua nozione pessimistica di "umorismo", quale lente d'ingrandimento capace di rivelare i lati più tragici dell'esistenza. Come esplica l'autore, l'umorismo si articola in due fasi. La prima è contrassegnata dall'"avvertimento del contrario" il quale, attraverso la mediazione della "riflessione, porta al "sentimento del contrario". L'"umorismo" di Pirandello e in grado di farci capire l'essenza nefasta dell'esistenza rendendoci sensibili sia alle stonature e alle ipocrisie dello spirito sia alle "maschere" che nascondono i segreti più intimi dell'essere umano (possiamo intuire che la vecchia imbellettata è cosí "mascherata" per non perdere l'amore di un uomo più giovane). Pietà e comicità sono ingredienti essenziali dell'umorismo pirandelliano.

Pirandello non accetta che Cervantes abbia voluto farci ridere raccontandoci le avventure di un povero folle. Egli si rifiuta di credere che il narratore cervantino abbia scordato il "lugar de la Mancha" dov'è nato il nostro "ingenioso hidalgo". E a questo riguardo Pirandello cita dal "prologo al lettore" cervantino: "Io non ho potuto contravvenire all'ordine naturale che vuole che "ogni cosa generi ciò che le somiglia"" (103). Secondo Pirandello, Cervantes avrebbe proiettato sullo schermo del libro la propria immagine rovesciata, per cui l'io dello scrittore si sinperimpone a quello del personaggio. Per Pirandello, Don Quijote è inequivocabilmente l'alter ego di Cervantes. Alcalá de Henares non può essere che il luogo di nascita di Don Quijote e il 1547 l'anno della sua nascita. In che altro modo, si domanda Pirandello, si potrebbe giustificare il fatto che Cervantes abbia voluto narrare le gesta di un personaggio "vivo e vero nel suo paese e nel suo tempo", e non le gesta di un paladino di Carlomagno nella Francia medievale. Come si spiega che Cervantes, continua Pirandello, abbia voluto mettere al centro della sua opera un personaggio anacronistico, ridicolo, solo, disperato, infelice nell'aspetto e nell'anima. Don Quijote e tutto il contrario di quello che dovrebbe essere un vero protagonista dei romanzi cavallereschi. La sola ragione valida per Pirandello e che il cavaliere errante sia il frutto di una mente che ha sofferto molto. Solo una persona afflitta da una cupa visione del mondo, scrive Pirandello, poteva immaginare tale figura.

Ma quali sono state le cause di tanto pessimismo? Pirandello ipotizza che l'umiliazione della sconfitta a Lepanto, cinque anni di prigionia in Algeri, le esperienze di soldato, l'orrore della morte e della violenza, vissuta in molte battaglie contro francesi e inglesi, devono aver ferito profondamente Cervantes.

L'umorismo, secondo Pirandello, era un mezzo che ha permesso a Cervantes di mettere in prospettiva le sue terribili esperienze. Sulla spinta della psicanalisi, lo scrittore italiano ritiene che l'umorismo abbia agito da meccanismo di difesa, capace di salvare Cervantes da un definitivo crollo psicologico. Attraverso gli occhi della sua fantasía Pirandello vede Cervantes rinchiuso nell'isolamento della cella, intento a riflettere sulla precarietà dei suoi ideali religiosi e patriottici: "egli si riconosce, egli si vede finalmente; si accorge che i giganti eran molini a vento e l'elmo di Mambrino un vil piatto da barbiere. Si vede, e ride di sé stesso. Ridono tutti i suoi dolori. Ah, folle.! folle! folle!" (103). Le parole di Pirandello evocano quelle di un altro scrittore influenzato dalla psicanalisi, Giuseppe Berto (1914-1978): e talvolta rido per disperazione, perchè l'ironia è la sola forma di comunicazione che mi rimane con un mondo assurdo" (Monterosso 65).

Siamo cosi pervenuti all'elemento focale della poetica pirandelliana, quello dell'autonomia del personaggio fittizio nei confronti del suo creatore. Per Pirandello, Don Quijote non è solo una finzione letteraria, una proiezione dell'io dello scrittore, bensi egli diventa fisicamente reale, un personaggio in carne ed ossa. Lo stesso avviene nel capolavoro cervantino, Don Quijote è pienamente cosciente della propria realtà fittizia. Questa importantissima analogia è stata messa in rilievo anche da Américo Castro: "Conviene aislar bien este tema del personaje consciente de su existencia dentro de la obra de arte" (379). Nel saggio sull'*Umorismo* leggiamo: "quando un poeta riesce veramente a dar vita a una sua creatura, questa vive indipendentemente dal suo autore, tanto che noi possiamo immaginarla in altre situazioni in cui lautore non pensò di collocarla, e vederla agire secondo le intime leggi della sua propria vita, leggi che neanche l'autore avrebbe potuto violare" (101).

Pirandello si immagina, anticipando un concetto caratterizzante della sua rpduzione letteraria successiva — pensiamo a opere quali *La tragedia d'un personaggio* (1911) e *Colloqui coi personaggi* (1915) — una conversazione tra l'autore e due personaggi fittizi, Cervantes, Don Quijote e El Cid.

L'e roe cavalleresco, il Cid Campeador, si materializza nella cella di Cervantes per beffarsi di Cervantes che non ha voluto narrare le sue geste, preferendo quelle ridicole di uno come Don Quijote che "volle vivere fuori del tempo e del mondo, nella leggenda o nel sogno dei poeti". El Cid non può capire come Cervantes abbia potuto ignorare un eroe che "potè far leggenda della sua storia" (104). Questa nozione dell'indipendenza del personaggio è, ripetiamo, fondamentale ai fini tematici e stilistici dell'estetica pirandelliana come si può vedere in *I sei personaggi in cerca d'autore*. Usando il termine di Sainte-Beuve, Pirandello parla della "plusvalenza futura" del personaggio, affermando che Sancio e Don Abbondio, in quanto personaggi, sono destinati a sopravvivere nel tempo molto a lungo dopo la scomparsa dei loro creatori (101).

In *Pirandello la follia* (1983) Enzo Gianola applica persuasivamente la tería psicoanalítica alla lettura de *Il fu Mattia Pascal*. È interessante notare che l'approccio di Gianola avvalora la nostra tesi dell'incidenza dell'archetipo donchisciottesco su pirandello. Il critico delinea i motivi centrali della poetica pirandelliana, crisi dell'io e ricerca dell'identità, attorno al tema della fuga dal contesto familiare e dell'assunzione di un nuovo nome, il tema del "chiamarsi". In realtà, sia in *Il fu Mattia Pascal* che nel libro di Cervantes, la realtà dell'io coincide con il modo in cui i protagonisti vengono chiamati. Il loro credo esistenziale potrebbe essere riassunto mediante la frase "mi chiamo dunque sono." Scrive infatti Gianola che in Pirandello "la certezza riguarda il nome, la consistenza anagrafica, non la consistenza ontológica . . . . Perdere il proprio nome significa propriamente perdersi, non esserci più" (81).

Gianola sottolinea nella sua analisi la conflittualità tra il protagonista e il padre. E' dunque per sottrarsi al proprio agressore, il padre, che Mattia Pascal assume l'identità di Adriano Meis. Scrive Gianola: "si è nella misura in cui si ha un nome, e si ha un nome perché ci viene dato: "chiamarsi" è una funzione della socialità, essere-per-gli-altri" (81). Il protagonista convalida questa interpretazione: "Una delle poche cose, anzi forse la sola ch'io sapessi di certo era questa : che mi chiamavo Mattia Pascal." Ma il tentativo del protagonista fallisce. Un nuovo nome non basta a soddisfare le proprie aspirazioni frustrate e a superare le durezze e i disinganni della vita. Accade lo stesso a Alonso Quijano, anch'egli dovrà accettare la sconfitta che il "falso io" di Don Quijote non può prevenire. Il tema del "chiamarsi" dunque conferma ulteriormente il legame fra Cervantes e Pirandello. Esso evidenzia un comune "modus narrandi" che permette ai due scrittori di esprimere attraverso immagini verbali l'alienazione del personaggio.[6]

Nel prologo del *Quijote* leggiamo un passo che conferma l'interpretazione psicoanalitica del Gianola: "Pero yo, que, aunque parezco padre, soy padrastro de Don Quijote" (9). È certo che la parola "hidalgo" sembra essere la contrazione di "hijo de algo," "figlio di qualcosa", o se si vuole "di qualcuno", e ritorna più volte nel testo; ricompare, per esempio, nel quarto capitolo, "cada uno es hijo de sus obras" (5, 4, 30). Il ripetersi dell'immagine della paternità, esplicitato dal titolo nobiliare "hidalgo," servirebbe, secondo la prospettiva freudiana, ad esprimere la ricerca di conforto familiare e lo smarrimento dell'identità di Don Quijote.

È lo stesso narratore cervantino a suggerirci questa lettura freudiana del *Quijote*, la dove, all'inizio del libro, egli non e capace di ricordare il luogo di nascita del protagonista. Don Quijote sembra voler regredire verso un mondo mitico dell'infanzia in cui sogno e realtà si compenetrano vicendevolmente: "En un lugar de la Mancha, de cuyo nombre no quiero acordarme, no ha mucho tiempo que vivía, un hidalgo" (5,1). Il narratore ci informa che esiste una certa confusione in merito all'esattezza del soprannome del nostro protagonista. Alcuni dicono che fosse "Quijada" o "Quesada" altri danno a intendere che si chiamava "Quejana." Ad ogni buon conto, il nostro hidalgo decide di cambiare il suo nome in "Quijote" che, nello spagnolo di Cervantes, descriveva quella parte dell'armatura che protegge la coscia e che probabilmente doveva avere per il lettore secentesco implicazioni sessuali (si veda Russell). Lo stesso suffisso "-ote" produce in spagnolo un effetto comico. Ma quello che importa per quanto concerne il nostro discorso è che Alonso Quijano, nel cambiare il proprio nome in onore di Amadis de Gaula e nel fuggire la famiglia, diventi un altro Mattia Pascal.

Pochi giorni dopo il rientro alla casa paterna, Don Quijote muore. La casa rappresenta, come per Mattia Pascal, il locus della sua esistenza. Lontani da essa, i due protagonisti subiscono sconfitte e umiliazioni. Nel passo seguente Gianola parla di Mattia Pascal, ma le sue parole potrebbero benissimo riferirsi a Don Quijote: "Mattia fugge in realtà da se stesso incapace, come l'orribile aspetto della vita con Romilda e la vedova Pescatore l'hanno costretto a verificare, di sostenere rapporti e ruoli. Ma esiste vita fuori dai ruoli e dai rapporti?" (89).

Mattia manifesta altri tratti tipicamente donchisciotteschi. Come Don Quijote, Mattia è un bibliofilo, un sognatore che vive in un mondo della fan-

---

[6] Sul tema del "chiamarsi" si veda Barthes in *Mythologies*.

tasia alienato dalla realtà circostante. Anche Mattia legge libri stravaganti e fuori moda che gli fanno perdere il senno: "Lessi di tutto un po', disordinatamente; ma libri, in ispecie, di filosofia. Pesano tanto: eppure, chi se ne ciba e se li mette in corpo, vive tra le nuvole. Mi sconcertarono il cervello, già di per se balzano" (Gianola 83). Mentre Don Quijote, ossessionato dal mondo cavalleresco, cerca l'avventura aggirandosi nelle pianure della Mancha, Mattia la cerca a Montecarlo sui tavoli verdi della roulette. La vincita al gioco, scrive Gianola, "è eretta contro il padre da parte di chi ha dovuto ricorrere al 'diavolo' non potendo disporre di nessuna sicurezza di sè" (93).

Giunti a questo punto, abbiamo visto che l'archetipo cervantino ben si attaglia alla problematica del *Fu Mattia Pascal*: non si può vivere senza un "io", conviene allora fingersi folli o morire (pensiamo a Enrico IV). Il tentivo di evasione attraverso una nuova identità è fallimentare sia in Pirandello che in Cervantes. Nemmeno il rifugiarsi in un falso io (Don Quijote) non può risolvere il dramma esistenziale di Alonso Quijano. Come Mattia egli torna al punto di partenza. Malato nel fisico e nello spirito Don Quijote, al suo rientro, lo aspetta la morte. Chiama allora intorno a sé la nipote, Sansón Carrasco, il prete, e il barbiere. Queste sono le sue ultime parole: "Dadme albricias, buenos señores, de que ya yo no soy don Quijote de la Mancha, sino Alonso Quijano, a quien mis costumbres me dieron renombre de 'Bueno' Ya soy enemigo de Amadis de Gaula y toda la infinita caterva de su linaje; ya me son odiosas todas las historias profanas de la adelante caballería" (II, 74). Nelle sue ultime parole possiamo cogliere la consapevolezza dell'atroce verità che affligge i personaggi pirandelliani: anche il falso io è un'illusoria fuga verso l'autenticitá. Nella vita non e possibile esistere senza un'identità. Ecco che la ricerca dell'io è vana, e meglio rifugiarsi nella finzione di un ruolo, oppure, come fa Don Quijote, lasciarsi morire.

L'interpretazione che Pirandello da della vita di Cervantes, però, non e convalidata dalla realtà storica dei fatti. Cervantes non era come Pirandello lo ritrae, un uomo neurotico e vinto. Cervantes era e rimase sempre un soldato, forte e fedele ai valori tradizionali della patria e della religione. È vero che Cervantes soffrì la mutilazione del corpo, ma rimase intatto nello spirito. La forza degli ideali dello scrittore spagnolo è evidente in Don Quijote, la cui vicenda serve da "exemplum" al lettore secentesco. Pertanto, egli esprime chiaramente il profondo sentimento religioso e la profonda dottrina che caratterizzano gli anni della Controriforma: Dio è il locus dell'esistenza e allontanandosi da esso, l'individuo smarrisce la via della ragione perdendosi nel labirinto della follia. Don Quijote infatti dopo innumerevoli disastrose avventure ritorna a casa per ricongiungersi con Dio e la famiglia. La nipote anticipa l'esito della sua storia quando ammonisce Don Quijote di non partire: "Quien le mete a vuestra merced señor tío, en esas pendencias? No será mejor estarse en su casa, y no irse por el mundo a buscar pan de trastrigo".

Durante gli anni fra il 1569 e il 1575, lo scrittore spagnolo visse a Roma e a Napoli dove non solo imparò l'italiano ma assimilò pure la cultura rinascimentale leggendo copiosamente, e in particolar modo, le opere del Tasso e dell'Ariosto. Cervantes, nel pieno dei vent'anni, era in Italia al servizio del cardinale Nunzio Acquaviva il quale lo mise in contatto con intellettuali italiani come il Robertelli, il Minturno e il Castelvetro. Cervantes si innamorò profondamente della cultura italiana. Il *Quijote* celebra questo amore per gli ideali rinascimentali, per l'Italia e, soprattutto, l'Ariosto. E Don Quijote incarna questi ideali. Possiamo ravvisare in lui una figura profondamente religiosa e cristiana. Don Quijote infatti esalta la fede cattolica sacrificando la propria vita che, come mette in risalto il libro, è messa sempre e completamente al servizio degli altri.

Nel *Quijote* ci sono precisi riferimenti testuali che testimoniano le esperienze di Cervantes in Italia. Nel capitolo 25 (IInda parte), le prime parole che Don Quijote rivolge a Mastro Pedro sono in italiano: "En esto, volvió Maese Pedro, y en una carreta venía el retablo, y el mono, grande y sin cola, con las posaderas de fieltro, pero no de mala cara; y apenas le vió don Quijote, cuando le preguntó: "Dígame vuesa merced, señor adivino: qué peje pillamo?" Anche se Cervantes tenta di tradurre la frase idiomatica "che pesci pigliamo" in spagnolo, l'autore non vuole nascondere l'origine italiana di questa espressione, ed infatti la leggiamo nel testo fra virgolette. Il verbo "pigliamo" echeggia il nome del personaggio in questione Mastro Pedro-Ginés de Pasamonte, anche conosciuto come Ginesillo de Parapilla. "Ginesillo" tradisce un modello napoletano, che è corroborata anche dall'appellativo di Ginés nella versione italiana: "Parapiglia". Cervantes aveva dunque tale dimistichezza con le sottigliezze linguistiche tra l'italiano e lo spagnolo da saper trovare una parola che si prestasse a un gioco di parole efficace in ambedue lingue. In spagnolo Parapilla suggerisce la parola "Pillar", cioè saccheggiare, il che ben si confà ad un galeotto come il nostro Ginés. D'altro canto, l'equivalente italiano, "parapiglia" ha una connotazione meno ladresca, e infatti ben si presta a descrivere lo stato generale di caos e di baraonda creato da Don Quijote nell'episodio del "retablo". Ricordiamo che il nostro eroe interviene sulla scena fittizia per salvare una damigella inseguita dai mori e, scambiando la realtà illusoria della scena con la realtà vivente, Don Quijote fa una strage di marionette. Ad ogni modo, entrambe le parole, sia "parapilla" che "parapiglia", servono perfettamente a evidenziare la duplicità morale di Ginés/Maese Pedro.

Possiamo osservare l'influsso italiano su Cervantes anche in capitolo 62 (IInda parte), lá dove Don Quijote si aggira per le strade di Barcellona. Fermatosi davanti a una tipografia, il nostro Cavaliere dalla Triste Figura decide di entrare. Il tipografo è intento a stampare un libro italiano, *Le bagatelle*, che ha tradotto in spagnolo con il titolo di *Los juguetes*. Conversando con il tipografo, Don Quijote rivela inaspettate qualità: è espertissimo in materie libresche, parla perfettamente l'italiano, e può recitare a memoria passi tratti dall'Ariosto. La loro lunga discussione copre tutti gli aspetti dell'editoria. E evidente che in questo episodio Cervantes si avvale del personaggio-alter ego per esprimere le proprie vedute sull'industria della stampa. Parla Don Quijote: "Yo — dijo don Quijote — sé algun tanto del toscano y me precio de cantar algunas estancias del Ariosto . . . Yo apostaré una buena apuesta que adonde diga en el toscano "piace" dice vuesa merced en castella place y adonde diga 'più' dice más, y el 'su' declara con arriba, y el 'giù' con abajo".

Ma è ora di avviarci verso la conclusione del nostro saggio. Sarebbe interessante allargare il discorso fino a coinvolgere altri scrittori che hanno adottato l'archetipo donchisciottesco. A titolo esemplificativo possiamo segnalare alcuni nomi di autori che altri potranno esaminare più attentamente. I protagonisti della trilogia dei *Nostri antenati* (1960) di Italo Calvino, per esempio, e in particolar modo il protagonista del *Visconte dimezzato* di Calvino, è un archetipo donchisciottesco. Calvino adatta il modello secondo la sua ideologia politica, pertanto la scissione dell'io-bene io-male del Visconte dimezzato è emblematica dello sfruttamento dell'individuo nella societa capitalistica.[7] Anche Leonardo Sciascia si appropria del modello donchisciottesco per scopi politici, pensiamo al breve dramma *L'onorevole* (1965). Qui non abbiamo un personaggio maschile, bensi' una donna, Assunta, moglie di Emanuele Frangipane, un professore liceale che persegue senza scrupoli la carriera politica riuscendo a diventare un "onorevole" democristiano. E' facile riconoscere la tipologia cervantina e pirandelliana che accomuna follia, comicità, tragedia. L'onestà di Assunta la porta alla follia, l'unica via d'uscita da una realtà familiare alienante.[8] Assunta cerca conforto recitando a memoria passi del capolavoro cervantino: "Ecco: dicevo che l'episodio del governatorato di Sancio e *La vita è sogno*

---

[7] Per avviare un esame del rapporto tra il motivo dei tarocchi e il retablo di Maese Pedro si veda JoAnn Cannon.

[8] Giovanna Jackson mette a fuoco il motivo dello scherzo in relazione al tema del Don Quijote.

dicono, in modo diverso, che il governare è beffa o sogno: dentro la beffa o il sogno della vita/E a me pare che Sancio ne sia uscito benissimo: non crede? "Andandomene nudo, come me ne vado in effetti, è chiaro che ho governato come un angelo'" (54).

Chiudiamo. Non abbiamo avuto la pretesa di dire tutto e in modo esauriente. Si spera solo che queste osservazioni possano essere state utili a ulteriori ricerche. Mi sembra però che abbiamo potuto individuare quella linea ideale che ricollega la narrativa moderna a Cervantes passando attraverso Pirandello. Finisco dunque con alcuni versi di Aldo Palazzeschi, tratti dalla poesia "L'incendiario", perchè essi sembrano decantare i tratti essenziali dell'archetipo donchisciottesco: "io brucio il mio primo esemplare,/e guardo avido quella fiamma,/e godo, e mi ravvivo,/ e sento salirmi il calore alla testa/ come se bruciasse il mio cervello."

Providence College

OPERE CITATE

AA.VV. *L'analisi del racconto*. Milano: Bompiani, 1969.

Barthes, Roland. *Mythologies*. Trans. Annette Lavers. New York: Hill and Wang, 1972.

Bell, Aubrey F.G. "Cervantes and the Renaissance." *Hispanic Review* 2 (1934), 89-101.

Cannon, JoAnn. *Italo Calvino: Writer and Critic*. Ravenna: Longo, 1981.

Castro, Américo. "Cervantes y Pirandello." *Hacia Cervantes* Madrid: Taurus, 1960.

Cervantes, Saavedra Miguel de. *El ingenioso hidalgo Don Quijote de la Mancha*. Ed. Américo Castro. Mexico: Editorial Porrúa, 1969.

Cipolla, Gaetano. "Pirandello: Don Quijote or Don Chisciotti." *Quaderni d'italianistica* 6 (1985) 111-116.

Croce, Alda. "Relazioni della letteratura italiana con la letteratura spagnola." *Letterature Comparate*. Milano: Marzorati, 1948. 4: 129-141.

Debenedetti, Giacomo. *Il romanzo del novecento*. Milano: Garzanti, 1976. 305-414.

Ferroni, Giulio. *Il comico nelle teorie contemporanee*. Roma: Bulzoni, 1974.

Getto, Giovanni. *Manzoni Europeo*. Milano: Mursia, 1971.

Gianola, Elio. *Pirandello la follia*. Genova: Il Melangolo, 1983.

Gieri, Manuela. "From Pascal to Mostarda: Pirandello 'Narrative within and beyond Modernism." *Forum Italicum*, 22 (1988), 176-186.

120

Jackson, Giovanna. *Leonardo Sciascia: 1956-1976*. Ravenna: Longo, 1981.

Lucente, Gregory. *Beautiful Fables*. Baltimore: John Hopkins UP, 1986.

Monterosso, Ferruccio. *Come leggere Il male oscuro di Giuseppe Berto*. Milano: Mursia, 1977.

Newberry, Wilma. *The Pirandellian Mode in Spanish Literature*. New York: State University of New York Press, 1973.

Pirandello, Luigi. *Saggi, poesie, scritti varii*. Milano: Mondadori, 1960. 17-160.

_____. *Tutti i romanzi*. Milano: Mondadori, 1984. 319-586.

Ricardou, Jean. *L'ordine e la disfatta*. Cosenza: Lerici, 1976.

Robert, Marthe. *L'antico e il nuovo*. Milano: Rizzoli, 1969.

Russell, P.E. *Cervantes*. New York: Oxford UP, 1985.

Sciascia, Leonardo. *L'onorevole*. Torino: Einaudi, 1965.

Scripta Humanistica

Directed by
BRUNO M. DAMIANI
The Catholic University of America
COMPREHENSIVE LIST OF PUBLICATIONS *

| 67. | *The Other Voices: Essays on Italian Regional Culture and Language.* Ed. John Staulo. | $35.50 |
| 68. | Mario Aste, *Grazia Deledda: Ethnic Novelist.* | $38.50 |

BOOK ORDERS

* Clothbound. *All book orders,* except library orders, must be prepaid and addressed to **Scripta Humanistica**, 1383 Kersey Lane, Potomac, Maryland 20854. *Manuscripts* to be considered for publication should be sent to the same address.

* 9 7 8 0 9 1 6 3 7 9 5 6 8 *